Asian Recipes for Dinner:

Easy, Quick and Healthy Asian Recipes Made Simple at Home.

(Asian Recipe Cookbook for Chicken, Beef, Vegetables, Fish, Rice Wine)

Henry Wilson

Legal & Disclaimer

The information contained in this book and its contents is not designed to replace or take the place of any form of medical or professional advice; and is not meant to replace the need for independent medical, financial, legal, or other professional advice or services, as may be required. The content and information in this book have been provided for educational and entertainment purposes only.

The content and information contained in this book have been compiled from sources deemed reliable, and it is accurate to the best of the Author's knowledge, information, and belief. However, the Author cannot guarantee its accuracy and validity and cannot be held liable for any errors and/or omissions. Further, changes are periodically made to this book as and when needed. Where appropriate and/or necessary, you must consult a professional (including but not limited to your doctor, attorney, financial advisor or such other professional advisor) before using any of the suggested remedies, techniques, or information in this book.

Upon using the contents and information contained in this book, you agree to hold harmless the Author from and against any damages, costs, and expenses, including any legal fees potentially resulting from the application of any of the information provided by this book. This disclaimer applies to any of the loss, damages or injury caused by the use and application, whether directly or indirectly, of any advice or information presented, whether for breach of contract, tort, negligence, personal injury, criminal intent, or under any other cause of action.

You agree to accept all risks of using the information presented in this book.

You agree that, by continuing to read this book, where appropriate and/or necessary, you shall consult a professional (including but not limited to your doctor, attorney, or financial advisor or such other advisor as needed) before using any of the suggested remedies, techniques, or information in this book.

CONTENTS

INTRODUCTION

The delectable recipes of this book are going to seize the attention of your taste buds. Always remember, good food means a good life and there is no other love in the world which is sincerer than food love. The incredible taste of rice wine adds vitality to the Asian dishes, and one glimpse of the mouth-watering recipes will definitely make you try all of them instantly.

An exclusive addition to this book includes the big difference between Rice Wine and Japanese Rice Wine which is commonly known as "Sake." There are recipes for vegetarians, but also some of the most elite, quintessential and delicious recipes for non-vegetarians as well. Chicken meals with rice wine, fish with rice wine, meat with rice wine, salad with rice wine and soup with rice wine are pervasive throughout the entire e-book and are scrumptious and yummy at the same time.

The fantastic rice wine has an exciting and thought-provoking history behind it which you should definitely understand. Knowing more about the flavor and its advantages helps us to recognize and cherish it in millions of ways possible. The flavor of rice wine is positively perceived and experienced while tasting the Asian and Korean cuisines which include rice wine.

Get yourself the best help with rice wine recipes, by purchasing this book, and make amazing and palatable Asian dishes, where food becomes your best friend. The best Chinese dishes include a hint of rice wine which makes the recipe succulent, flavorsome and gratifying. The best of them are revealed and conveyed here in the easiest way possible.

ABOUT RICE WINE IN ASIAN CUISINE

Rice wine is generally used in South Asian, Southeast Asian and East Asian countries for cooking and it is also consumed as a beverage. Dissimilar from varieties of wine in the market this one is something different and unique. Most of the wines which are available in the market are made up of fermented fruit juice or molasses. Rice wine extracts from the acidulated, fermented mucilaginous rice. The method includes the transformation of sugar into alcohol. This process is entirely completed by yeasting.

When comparing wines made from fruits and grapes, rice wine has more alcohol content. Studies show that it has 18 to 25% of alcohol, whereas traditional wine contains only 10 to 20% alcohol. Therefore, consuming an excess quantity of rice wine can cause inebriation. People drinking an excessive amount of rice wine would show early signs of a hangover, nausea, loss of muscle control, etc., similar to that of consuming alcohol.

Rice wine has a delectable and luscious taste, and it is used in a variety of Asian and Chinese recipes. It adds an unfathomable and profound relish in the dishes. Rice wine is usually sweet. Some of them are very popular as a beverage.

BENEFITS OF RICE WINE

With an amazing and delicious flavor, rice wine has mind-boggling benefits for health. Usually, people do not consider the advantages of wine just because it is 'wine.' Rice Wine breaks the stereotype. The following are some the little-known but incredible benefits of rice wine.

- **Improves blood circulation:** Rice wine has excellent properties in controlling fatty peroxide in blood. As a result, it can prevent the formation of bad cholesterol building up on blood vessel walls. It can enhance blood circulation and heart health.

- **Enhances immunity:** The presence of amino acids in Rice wine helps to improve immunity. It can control the damaging effect of free radicals and can boost the immune system.

- **Controls inflammation:** The peptide contents in the Rice wine can help to reduce inflammation, which is commonly found in the inner colon lining. The presence of high nutritional substances in Rice wine can effectively offer protection from inflammation.

- **Acts like a probiotic:** Rice wine has lactic acid in it. Because of the presence of this, it is considered as probiotic, and that's why it is perfect for increasing and enhancing the health of the stomach.

- **Tumor deterrent:** People who suffer from tumors should consider rice wine for a small step towards the cure. Rice wine decreases the size of tumors and deters bacteria that causes cancer.

- **Anti-bacterial properties:** The presence of high anti-bacterial properties can protect your body from bacterial infections such as Staphylococcus aureus, and Bacillus subtilis. It is also effective in resisting Escherichia coli and Pseudomonas aeruginosa.

- **UV ray protection:** Rice wine is a fantastic beverage as it protects you from harmful and dangerous ultraviolet rays of the sun.

- **Anti-aging:** Studies in Korea have revealed its contribution to preventing premature aging tendencies. Rice Wine can promote skin health when applied directly on the skin, as it can stimulate the sensory neurons of the cells. It can also improve skin elasticity.

What is Rice Wine?

As the name suggests, rice wine is a beverage made of rice. Rice wine is made by fermenting glutinous rice. During the fermentation process, the rice starch is converted into sugars. The presence of microbes in the molasses acts as the enzymes to convert starch to sugar. Upon aging, the pH value of the liquid will show a considerable reduction, which indicates the increase of acidity, as a result of yeasting. When the acidity increases, the alcohol content also starts to build-up. The longer it is left to age, the more alcohol content it produces.

Rice wine is an alcoholic beverage which is used in numerous serving dishes. It has 18-25% of alcohol content which makes it luscious. There are so many types of rice wine available in the market, and some of the famous ones are Mirin (Japan), Sake (Japan), Shaoxing (China), Handia (India), Tuak & Lihing (Malaysia), Tapai or Brem (Indonesia/Bali), Makgeolli (Korea), Lao Lao (Laos), Ruou can (Vietnam), etc.

The flavor of the wine can vary depending on the process and types of rice used for making the wine. However, the rice wine is sweet in taste generally. The most famous wines are Chinese rice wine Shaoxing, Japanese rice wine mirin and sake.

One can also try to make rice wine at the convenience of their home. Try this simple yet effective method to make rice wine.

General Method:

1. Cook the rice as you usually do.

2. After the rice has completely cooked, take it out on a baking sheet.

3. Take a small bowl and break up the yeast.

4. In a container place a spoon of rice (room temperature) and then place some yeast on it.

5. Fill the container by repeating the process till the rice and yeast have layered completely.

6. Now, secure the container tightly and leave it for 5-6 days. Place it in a warm space.

7. The yeast will slowly and gradually break down the pieces of rice, and some liquid will evolve as a result. The liquid precipitating is the rice wine in the making.

8. After 2-3 weeks, the wine is ready to use. Strain it through a cloth and store it in the refrigerator.

How to use Rice Wine?

Apart from being a fantastic and delicious beverage, rice wine is an excellent ingredient for a variety of dishes. Every country has its own rice wine with a unique flavor. However, the taste of rice wine from Korea, India, China, and Vietnam stand very close to each other. On a broad canvass, these are categorized as sweet wine and have a minimal difference in their taste.

One can definitely take the considerable advantage of the sweetness of rice wine to give a toothsome and piquant flavor to a succulent and mellow dish. Rice wine can be used for both veg and non-veg dishes, but it is excellent to use with meat recipes, especially when you want to marinade. The alcohol content makes the meat soft and also lets the spices/marinade mix get absorbed into the meat. Apart from marinating, rice wine can also use in salads, and to make sauces.

Taste of Rice Wine

The taste of rice wine is more on the sweet side than sour. It is sweet and undoubtedly very delicious. Mostly rice wines have a sweet taste except some which have a high content of alcohol in them. As per research, Indian, Chinese, Vietnamese and Korean rice wines are luscious and are used all across the world to make tasty dishes. The taste is just on point and perfect for those Asian cuisines and many more Chinese dishes.

Find the alternatives:

One can always have access to the substitutes of rice wine. One of the most commonly used alternatives for rice wine is Sherry. Go for sherry when you don't have rice wine instead of including rice wine in the ingredient list and your dish.

To combat the insufficiency of rice wine, Sherry is a perfect match for your recipe. If sherry is also not in your Kitchen's closet, then you can definitely go for a dry white wine. It is pretty similar to rice wine and gives an amazing and delicious taste to your dishes.

While rice wine is an excellent ingredient for Asian and Chinese cuisines, it should not be interchangeably used with rice vinegar for any purpose, because both are different.

COOKING RICE WINE & ALCOHOLIC JAPANESE RICE WINE 'SAKE'

Though Rice wine and sake are both grain alcohols fermented from rice and both have some identical characters, only the process of making them is different. Rice wine beverage, is fermented and distilled from rice, whereas the Japanese sake is produced by fermentation only. Since the process is different, both have unique characters, taste, and flavor. Both are used for cooking and consumption as a beverage.

TYPES OF RICE WINE

Luscious wine is part of many cultures across the world. Celebrations become lavish with the sweetness and fragrance of a variety of wines. Rice wine is different from other wines for several reasons. Firstly, it is the fermented extract of rice grains. Hence, many prefer to call it 'rice beer' than rice wine. The alcohol content of rice wine is between 20-25%. Secondly, the rice wine is primarily a seasoning element and cooking ingredient for many Asian dishes and then a drink.

The rice wine is popular among the Chinese and the South Asian communities like Korea and Japan. They serve rice wine as a beverage drink and use it as a seasoning ingredient. Though the Chinese introduced rice wine to the South Asians, both the communities have their unique process of preparation and use. We shall look into the varied applications of rice wine in the Chinese, Korean and Japanese cuisines as well as their preparation methods.

RICE WINE IN CHINESE CUISINE

PREPARATION OF THE MIJIU:

Cooking wines are an integral part of Chinese dishes, and it gives a unique flavor to the food. The 'Mijiu' wine or white wine is the popular wine among other cooking wines used in Chinese dishes. The 'Shaoxing rice wine' is also a Mijiu wine and has a flavor that would keep away the redolent smell of meat, fish, and seafood and enhances the dish with a delicate aroma.

It is also used as a chief cooking ingredient in casual Chinese dishes like stir-fry vegetables, desserts, stews, and soups instead of water. Chicken soups, Hongshaorou (cooked pork belly) are among the non-vegetarian savory dishes which use rice wine as an essential ingredient. Desserts are also made delicious with the Mijiu. We shall look into the preparation method of Mijiu and Shaoxing rice wine.

Fermented sticky glutinous rice is the basic ingredient for making make both the wines. The rice must be rinsed well and soaked in hot water for some time. The rice must be sieved and steamed well. The steamed rice must be cooled well before fermentation. Later crush the yeast into the rice to catalyze fermentation. Keep it in an airtight container in a warm environment. After a few days, we can find the liquid accumulated towards the bottom of the container. The liquid needs to strain before using, and that is our Mijiu.

PREPARATION OF SHAOXING RICE WINE:

The Shaoxing rice wine also needs the fermentation of white raw rice which is steamed and cooled like the Mijiu rice wine. Later, by adding the required quantity of black raisins and brown sugar to the rice, it is kept in a container. Add the lemon juice along with the yeast and close the container tightly. Stir the solution every day once for next eighteen days. Later transfer the solution into another vessel and keep it closed for a week, unstirred. The Shaoxing wine is ready to be served.

RICE WINE IN JAPANESE CUISINE

The Japanese food culture has rice wine or 'Mirin' as the cooking wine as well as a beverage drink. It is more a flavoring agent or syrup. The Mirin preparation takes nearly one year. Just like the Mijiu, savory as well as dessert dishes, are flavored and enriched with the Japanese Mirin. Then we have Sake wine as the next most popular in the list. First, we shall investigate the preparation of Sake wine.

PREPARATION OF SAKE RICE WINE:

Sake's rice is mixed with water and allowed to ferment by using 'Koji.' The same mix is added to for 3 consecutive days and is later mashed and kept for another 30 days. The filtered and pasteurized Sake is ready to be relished.

PREPARATION OF MIRIN:

The rice preparation of the Mirin is the same as that of Chinese rice wines. Mirin is usually made with the fermentation of steamed rice using the Koji molds. The 'Shochu' or the distilled alcohol mixed with the solution should be kept for nearly 60 days to form Mirin. For making homemade Mirin, sugar, and water added to the sake wine. Nowadays many companies make these beverages and they are also readily available in the market.

RICE WINE IN KOREAN CUISINE

PREPARATION OF MAKGEOLLI:

The Korean people use the 'Makgeolli' rice wine or the 'Soju' like the Chinese counterparts. Makgeolli is loved for its sweetness as well as sourness. The liquid is mainly used with non-vegetarian spicy dishes as a drink. Just like the fermentation of Mijiu rice, the Nuruk yeast is added to Korean sweet rice to make Makgeolli. Nuruk promotes the growth of molds in the solution, and the yeast will work as a catalyzer. The liquid will be perfect after 8-9 days and can be served after straining well. The Makgeolli is usually used as an ingredient in marinades. They are used for seasoning and also as a chief ingredient for desserts.

PREPARATION OF SOJU RICE WINE:

Distilling alcohol from the fermented rice grains is the common process for making Soju rice wine. This popular beverage has led in the past, to the shortage of rice in South Korea. Later, people have started preparing Soju from sweet potatoes as well as tapioca. The steamed potatoes and tapioca have to be mashed well before being used for fermentation. The mashed mix is subjected to fermentation. The solution can be strained after several days and will be ready to serve. Soju is mostly a drink than a pure wine used as a seasoning agent or ingredient.

The notable fact is that most of the rice wine preparation undergoes an identical process. The difference is in the type of rice, fermentation starter, amount of sugar and the days of which it is kept for preparation. However, each wine has different tastes, and they have different flavors when added to the various dishes. They are culture-specific as well as unique.

All the above-discussed rice wines have health benefits. The acceleration of blood circulation, high metabolism and digestion are the primary advantages of rice wines. Moreover, as suggested earlier, the flavoring aspect of these rice wines in Asian cuisines are unique and delicious.

TOP RICE WINE RECIPES IN KOREAN CUISINE

1. VEGAN KOREAN KIMCHI FRIED RICE

Preparation time: 10 minutes | Cooking: 10 minutes | Serving: 2

Ingredients:

- Red onion, diced - ¼ cup
- Rice wine - 1 tablespoon
- Garlic, minced – 1 tablespoon
- Vegetable oil – 1 tablespoon
- Kimchi, nicely chopped - ½ cup
- Ginger, finely grated - 1½ teaspoons
- Cooked white rice (one day old) – 1 cup

- Sesame oil - ½ tablespoon
- Sodium soy sauce – 2 tablespoons
- White sugar – 2 tablespoons
- Kimchi brine – 2 tablespoons
- Black pepper ground – as required
- Salt – taste

Cooking direction:

- Take a large nonstick pan, pour oil into it and heat on medium temperature.
- When oil becomes hot, add garlic, ginger and red onion.
- Stir occasionally and cook until the onion becomes tender. It will take approximately 3 minutes.
- Now change the heat setting to high and add kimchi and rice wine.
- Add cooked rice, kimchi brine, soy sauce, and sugar and sesame oil.
- Continue heating for about 5 minutes and stir well.
- Do not let the food stick on the bottom of the pan.
- When the cooking is over, serve it hot.
- Season with pepper and salt to your taste.

Approximate Nutritional Values:

Calories: 275 | Carbohydrates: 41.6g | Fat: 10.6g | Cholesterol: 0mg | Protein: 4.1g | Sodium: 961mg | Potassium: 210mg | Sugars: 14g

2. SLOW COOKER KOREAN CHICKEN

Preparation: 10 minutes | Cooking: 6 hours | Servings: 4

Ingredients:

Chicken section:

- Chicken thighs – 2 pounds
- Onion, diced – 1 large
- Potatoes, peeled and diced – 2
- Mushrooms quartered – 6
- Carrots, peeled & cut into chunks – 2 large
- Garlic, minced – 5 cloves
- Ginger, skinned and minced – 1 piece
- Chilies, whole, dried – 2

The sauce section:

- Rice wine – 3 tablespoons
- Oyster sauce – 2 tablespoons
- Soy sauce - ⅓ cup
- Brown sugar (dark) – 4 tablespoons
- Pepper ground - ¼ teaspoon

Garnish section:

- Scallions – 5
- Sesame oil – 2 teaspoons
- Sesame seeds (toasted) – 2 tablespoons
- Rice/noodles

For thickening:

- Corn flour (mixed with water) – 2 tablespoons

Cooking directions:

- In a slow cooker, put vegetables, ginger, chilies, garlic, and chicken.
- In a medium bowl mix all the sauce ingredients and pour over the items in the slow cooker.
- Set the cooker to 6-hour slow cooking.
- Add corn flour mix half an hour before the end of the cooking and stir slowly.
- Cook until the sauce becomes thick.
- Drizzle sesame oil before serving.
- Garnish with chopped scallions and toasted sesame seeds.
- Serve hot.

Approximate Nutritional Values:

Calories: 742 | Cholesterol: 222mg | Fat: 42g | Carbs: 43g | Dietary fiber: 5g | Sugars: 16g | Protein: 45g | Sodium: 1544mg | Potassium: 1342mg

Top Rice Wine Recipes in Japanese Cuisine

1. Japanese Chicken-Scallion Rice Bowl

Preparation: 15 minutes | Cooking: 20 minutes | Servings: 4

Ingredients:

- Skinless, boneless chicken breasts (½" cut size) – 8 ounces
- Brown rice (Instant) - 1½ cups
- Sodium chicken broth (reduced) – 1 cup
- Rice wine – 1 tablespoon

- Sugar - 1½ tablespoons
- Egg – 1 large
- Egg whites – 2 large
- Scallions, thinly sliced – 6

Cooking:

- Cook the instant brown rice as per package instructions.
- In a medium saucepan, pour broth, soy sauce, rice wine, and sugar.
- Heat on medium-high temperature until it starts to boil.
- Once boiled, reduce the heat to medium-low.
- In a medium bowl, stir egg and egg white and mix it thoroughly.
- In the simmering broth, put the chicken.
- Pour the beaten egg over chicken.
- Do not stir.
- Spread scallions on top of the chicken.
- When the egg becomes firm, stir with chopsticks.
- Serve the rice into 4 bowls and serve chicken on top of it.

Approximate Nutritional Values:

Calories: 257 | Carbohydrates: 34g | Fat: 4g | Protein: 19g | Cholesterol: 78mg | Sugars: 7g | Fiber: 2g | Sodium: 489mg | Potassium: 296mg

2. Japanese Salmon Kasu

Preparation: 10 minutes | Cooking: 10 minutes | Servings: 4

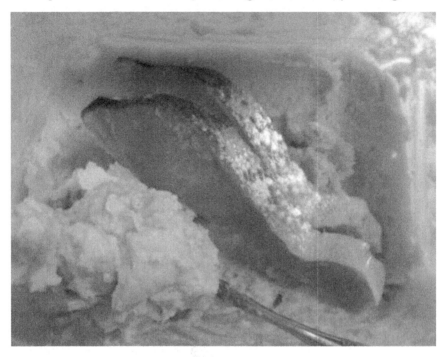

Ingredients:

- Salmon fillets – 6 ounces
- Rice wine - ¼ cup
- White miso - ¼ cup
- Water - ¼ cup
- Canola oil – 1 teaspoon
- Kasu - ⅓ cup
- Brown sugar (dark) – 1 tablespoon
- Soy sauce with low sodium – 1 tablespoon

Cooking instructions:

- Take a saucepan and pour sake into it.

- Heat on low temperature for 5 minutes.
- Remove sake from the pan.
- In a food processor put sake, soy sauce, water, miso, kasu, and blend.
- Let it form to a thick consistency.
- Now take a large baking pan and spread the paste over it.
- Place the salmons over the paste.
- Spread the remaining paste over the salmons.
- Cover it and refrigerate for 10-48 hours.
- Preheat the oven to medium-high temperature.
- Now scrape the kasu paste from the salmon and pat dry the fish. You can use a paper towel to dry the fish.
- Before broiling, slightly spread oil on salmon.
- Now place it in the oven for 10-12 minutes and broil it.
- Serve hot.

Approximate Nutritional Values:

Calories: 361.6 | Carbohydrates: 13g | Protein: 40.8g | Fat: 11.7g | Cholesterol: 90.1mg | Fiber: 0.9g

TOP RICE WINE RECIPES IN CHINESE CUISINE

1. WATERCRESS WITH RICE WINE-OYSTER SAUCE

Preparation: 25 | Cooking: 25 | Servings: 4

Ingredients:

For Rice Wine-Oyster Sauce:

- Rice wine – 1 tablespoon
- Vegetarian oyster sauce – 2 teaspoons
- Sugar - ¼ teaspoon
- Salt – to taste

For Watercress Stir-Fry:

- Canola oil – 2 tablespoons
- Garlic, minced – 2 cloves
- Sesame oil – 1 teaspoon
- Watercress – 24 cups

Cooking instructions:

- In a medium bowl, combine rice wine, sugar, oyster sauce, and salt.

Watercress preparation:

- Take large skillet and heat over high temperature.
- Pour canola oil into the skillet and swirl it.
- When the oil becomes hot, add garlic and stir-fry for about 10-15 seconds.
- Now add watercress and stir continuously.
- Add rice wine sauce to the pan.
- Continue frying approximately 2 minutes or until the watercress becomes tender. Be careful to maintain the greenness of the watercress.
- Add sesame oil.
- Discard garlic and serve hot.

Nutritional values:

Calories: 104 | Carbohydrates: 4g | Protein: 5g | Fiber: 1g | Fat: 8g | Cholesterol: 0mg | Sodium: 285mg | Potassium: 674mg | Sugars: 1g

2. CHINESE SEARED PORK WITH RICE WINE

Preparation: 15 | Cooking: 15 | Serving: 2

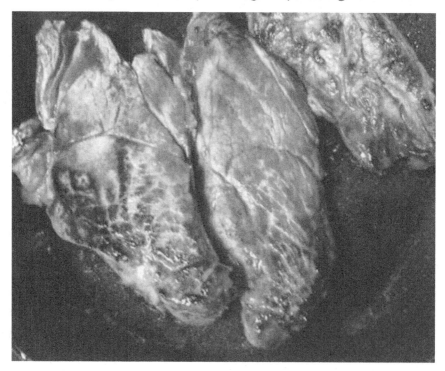

Ingredients:

- Lean pork, thinly sliced - ¼ pound
- Onion, diced – 1 green
- Rice wine – 2 tablespoons
- Vegetable oil – 2 tablespoons
- Ginger, fresh (thin slice) - ½" piece
- Soy sauce (low sodium) – 1 teaspoon
- Soy sauce (dark) - ½ teaspoon
- Sugar - ⅓ teaspoon
- Sesame oil – 1 teaspoon
- Salt – to taste

Cooking directions:

- In a large wok, heat oil over medium-high temperature.
- When the oil becomes hot, add ginger and fry.
- Add pork, dark soy sauce, sugar, salt, soy sauce and cook for about 10 minutes.
- Stir frequently.
- Pour sesame oil, rice wine, green onion and reduce the heat.
- Continue cooking until the pork becomes tender.
- Once the cooking is over, serve hot.

Nutritional values:

Calories: 322 | Carbs: 2.2g | Fat: 29.7g | Protein: 9.4g | Cholesterol: 41mg | Sodium: 838mg | Potassium: 197mg | Sugars: 1g

50 ASIAN RECIPES

Asian Chicken Meals

1. Teriyaki Chicken – Asian Style

Preparation: 5 minutes | Cooking: 12 minutes | Servings: 4

Ingredients:

- Skinless, boneless chicken breasts cut into pieces – 1 pound.
- Salt – to taste
- Broccoli Florets – 2 cups
- Oil – 1 Tablespoon
- Sliced strips of – 1 Bell paper
- Sesame seeds (for garnishing) – as required
- Cooked brown rice – 2 cups
- Dark or Light Soy Sauce – ¼ cup
- Pepper – as needed
- Meal preparation containers - 4

Preparation of Teriyaki Sauce:

- Soy sauce (light) - ¼ cup
- Honey – 2 tablespoons
- Rice wine – 2 tablespoons
- Cornstarch – 1 tablespoon
- Minced garlic – 1 clove
- Sesame oil – ½ teaspoon
- Ground ginger – ¼ teaspoon

Cooking directions:

- Heat a large pan in medium or high temperature.
- Add chicken
- Sprinkle salt and pepper and cook for about 3 minutes until the chicken color changes.
- Put all the ingredients in a bowl for preparing teriyaki sauce.
- Mix the chicken with teriyaki sauce and sauté it for 4-5 minutes until it gets thick.
- When the sauce becomes thick, remove the chicken from the pan.
- Now put broccoli florets along with bell pepper to the pan.
- Sauté for 3-4 minutes until the bell pepper becomes soft.
- Transfer the chicken and bell pepper mix into four food containers.
- Serve half cup rice to each container.
- Garnish with sesame seeds and close the container.
- You can refrigerate it for four days.

Approximate Nutritional values:

Calories: 235 | Carbohydrate: 15.2g | Protein: 28.2g | Sugars: 9.9g | Fat: 6.8g |Cholesterol: 82.8mg | Sodium: 938.1mg

2. CHICKEN AND BOK CHOY – AMERICAN STYLE

Preparation: 5 minutes | Cooking: 10 minutes | Servings: 4

Ingredients:

Sauce Preparation:

- Honey – 6 tablespoons
- Rice wine vinegar – 1 tablespoon
- Fresh ginger grated – ½ teaspoon
- Minced Garlic – 2 cloves
- Gluten-free soy sauce (less sodium) – 2 tablespoons

Stir Fry Preparation:

- Sesame oil – 1 teaspoon
- Skinless, boneless chicken breasts, 1" cut size – 1 pound
- Washed fresh bok choy, 1" strip piece – 1 head

- Peeled slices of carrots – ½ cup
- Diced green onions – 5-6
- Sesame seeds – 1 tablespoon
- Chopped cilantro – ¼ cup

Cooking directions:

- Take a bowl, mix all the ingredients for the sauce and keep it aside.
- In a large wok add sesame oil and heat it over medium temperature.
- Add chicken breasts in the wok and cook for 5-7 minutes.
- After that, add green onions, bok choy, and carrots.
- Continue heating and stir for about 3 minutes.
- Add the prepared sauce and cook until the chicken and vegetables get the appropriate coating.
- Garnish with cilantro.
- Serve hot.

Approximate Nutritional values:

Calories: 226 | Carbohydrate: 17g | Protein: 28g | Sugars: 12g | Fat: 5g |Cholesterol: 72mg | Sodium: 292mg | Potassium: 1097mg | Dietary Fiber: 3g

3. Chicken Wings – Chinese Style

Preparation: 20 minutes | Cooking: 30 minutes | Servings: 6

Ingredients:

- Boneless Chicken Breasts Strips – 2-3 pounds
- Egg – 1
- Water – 2 tablespoons for making the egg wash
- Flour – 1 cup
- Black pepper – ½ teaspoon
- Cayenne pepper – ¼ teaspoon
- Ground ginger – 3 tablespoons
- Soy Sauce – 4 tablespoons
- Rice wine vinegar – 4 teaspoons
- Water – ¼ cup
- Toasted sesame seed oil – 2 tablespoons
- Hot chili paste – 2 tablespoons

- Cornstarch – 2 teaspoons
- Minced garlic – 3 cloves
- Fresh ginger grated - 3 tablespoons
- Salt – to taste

Cooking directions:

- Mix 1 cup flour with cayenne pepper, ground ginger and black pepper and keep aside.
- Add salt to taste with the mix.
- Now take the chicken piece and dip in the egg wash and roll in the flour mix.
- Place the coated chicken on a slightly oil sprinkled banking sheet.
- Sprinkle some oil on top of the chicken pieces.
- Place the chicken in the baking oven at 375 degrees Celsius for about 30 minutes.
- Flip it after 10-15 minutes to make sure it bakes appropriately on both sides.
- Prepare sauce in the meantime carefully and make a caramel base to avoid overheating.
- Make a mixture of 4 tablespoons soy sauce, ¼ cup of water, four tablespoons rice wine vinegar, sesame seeds oil, two teaspoons cornstarch with a perfect blend of minced garlic and grated ginger.
- Add salt to taste and keep it aside.
- Boil 1 cup of sugar with ¼ cups of water in a medium pan.
- Caramel will give the color of light amber over the medium temperature and will provide the fresh odor of caramel.
- Now stir the cornstarch mixture and add to the hot caramel.
- At this stage take proper care as the sauce will foam up.
- Mix it well at a low temperature.
- Pour the mix over the cooked chicken.

- Serve hot along with steamed rice.

Nutritional value:

Calories: 429 | Carbohydrate: 46g | Protein: 36g | Sugars: 33g | Fat: 10g |Cholesterol: 127mg |Sodium: 1874mg | Potassium: 698mg | Dietary Fiber: 1g

4. LEMON CHICKEN – CHINESE STYLE

Preparation: 30 minutes |Cooking: 20 minutes | Servings: 4

Ingredients:

- Skinless chicken breast halves (boneless) – 6 ounces
- Brown Rice (long grain) – 1 cup
- Rice wine – 4 tablespoons
- Soy Sauce – 2 tablespoons
- Cornstarch – ½ teaspoon
- Dark Brown Sugar – 2 tablespoons
- Lemon Juice – 2 teaspoons
- Kosher Salt – ¼ teaspoon
- Black Pepper – ¼ teaspoon
- Canola oil – 2 teaspoons
- Trimmed broccolini – 1 pound

Cooking directions:

- Preheat your over to 400 degrees Fahrenheit.
- Cook brown rice as per the instructions on the packet.
- Mix soy sauce and cornstarch in a pan.
- Add brown sugar, rice wine, and lemon juice together.
- Boil it for a minute or until the mix becomes thick.
- Take salt and pepper and sprinkle over the chicken.
- Now take ovenproof skillet and heat to medium-high temperature.
- Pour canola oil and spread it in the pan evenly.
- Put chicken in the pan and cook about 4 minutes.
- Flip it and drop one tablespoon soy sauce over the chicken.
- Start baking in 400 degrees Fahrenheit for about eight minutes.
- Once the chicken has cooked, put the chicken on a cutting board.
- After cooling for 5 minutes cut it in slices.
- Now take a large saucepan and add water.
- Bring to boil and put broccolini for 3 minutes.
- Add water to the large pan and add broccolini for 3 minutes or until it becomes tender.
- Once it becomes tender, drain and keep ready for serving.
- Serve ½ cup rice in every four bowls.
- On top of the rice serve chicken and broccolini 4 ounces each.
- Drizzle one tablespoon soy sauce mixture over each serving.

Nutritional value:

Calories: 429 | Saturated fat: 1.2g | Fat: 10g | Sodium: 578mg

5. KOREAN CHICKEN

Preparation: 15 minutes | Cooking: 10 minutes | Servings: 4

Ingredients:

Marinade:

- Rice wine: 2 teaspoons
- Soy sauce: 1 tablespoon
- Cornstarch: 1½ teaspoons
- 1-inch cubes of chicken breasts (boneless & skin removed) – 1 Pound

Sauce:

- Black vinegar (Chinese): 1 teaspoon
- Hoisin sauce: 1 teaspoon
- Soy sauce: 1 teaspoon
- Sugar: 2 teaspoons
- Cornstarch: 1 teaspoon
- Ground Sichuan pepper: ½ teaspoon

- Vegetable oil: 2 tablespoons
- Sesame oil: 1 teaspoon
- Red chili (Dried): 8-10
- Sliced and sorted scallions: 3
- Minced garlic: 2 cloves
- Minced ginger: 1 teaspoon
- Roasted peanuts (unsalted): ¼ Cup

Cooking directions:

- Mix soy sauce, cornstarch, and rice wine in a bowl.
- Combine until the cornstarch dissolves in the mix.
- Put chicken to the mix and coat the mix thoroughly.
- Keep it aside for 10 minutes.
- Now let us prepare the sauce. Pour and stir black vinegar, soy sauce, sesame oil, Sichuan pepper, cornstarch, sugar, and hoisin sauce in a medium bowl and keep it aside.
- Make sure to dissolve the cornstarch and sugar thoroughly in the sauce.
- Heat a wok in high temperature.
- When it becomes hot add peanut oil and spread it in the base evenly.
- Stir-fry the chilies for 30 seconds or until the chilies start to become black, add the chicken, let it cook for 2-3 minutes carefully.
- Keep on the extractor fan, if the chili smoke bothers you.
- Now add garlic, scallion whites, and ginger and stir for 30 seconds.
- Add sauce and combine with the ingredients.
- Now add peanuts and continue cooking for 2-3 minutes.
- Scatter scallion greens while serving.
- Serve hot.

Nutritional value:

Calories: 357 | Carbohydrate: 9g | Protein: 27g | Fat: 23g |
Protein: 27g | Sodium: 392mg | Fiber: 2g | Cholesterol: 73mg

6. CHINESE CHICKEN

Preparation: 15 minutes | Cooking: 10 minutes | Servings: 3

Ingredients:

- Boneless, skinless chicken thighs: 3
- Rice Wine Vinegar: 1 tablespoon
- Liquid aminos: 1½ tablespoons
- Chili garlic sauce: ½ tablespoon
- Coconut oil: 2 tablespoons
- Raw cashews: ¼ cup
- White onion: ¼ medium
- Green bell pepper: ½
- Ground ginger: ½ teaspoon
- Minced garlic: 1 tablespoon
- Sesame oil: 1 tablespoon
- Green onions chopped: 1 tablespoon

- Sesame seeds: 1 tablespoon
- Salt and Pepper – to taste

Cooking directions:

- Heat the pan in the low temperature and roast the cashews until they become slightly brown. Once they become brown remove and keep aside.
- Cut the chicken in 1-inch cubes.
- Chop the pepper and onion in a large size equal to chicken cubes.
- In the pan, heat the coconut oil at high temperature.
- Add chicken thighs and cook it for 5 minutes.
- When the chicken is cooked well, sprinkle pepper, onions, garlic, and seasoning and cook for 2-3 minutes.
- Add rice wine, liquid aminos, and continue cooking until the liquid thickens.
- Serve with drizzled sesame oil and sprinkled with sesame seeds.

Nutritional value:

Calories: 333.3 | Carbohydrate: 8g | Protein: 22.6g | Fat: 24g |Fiber: 1.3g

7. WOK CHICKEN– ITALIAN STYLE

Preparation: 10 minutes | Cooking: 25 minutes | Servings: 4

Ingredients:

Chicken preparation:

- Skin removed boneless chicken breasts: 4
- Olive oil: 1 tablespoon
- Garlic powder: 1 teaspoon
- Ground pepper: to taste
- Salt: to taste

White Wine Sauce preparation:

- Unsalted butter: 1 tablespoon
- Diced yellow onion: 1 large
- Minced garlic: 3 cloves
- Shaoxing rice wine: ½ cup
- Thyme: 1 teaspoon

- Heavy Cream: ½ cup
- Chopped Parsley - few

Cooking directions:

Chicken preparation:

- Put chicken in a medium bowl and season it with garlic and pepper.
- Add salt to taste
- Heat olive oil in a large wok for 2-3 minutes.
- Add the seasoned chicken to the wok and cook for about 6 minutes.
- When one side becomes golden brown, flip it and continue cooking for another 6 minutes.
- Now transfer the cooked chicken to a plate and cover and keep aside.

White Wine Sauce preparation:

- Heat the same wok on medium flame.
- Add butter and let it melt down.
- Now add the onion and cook for 3 minutes or until it becomes translucent.
- Sprinkle the seasoning such as pepper, and garlic and cook until you can smell the fragrance.
- Add salt to taste.
- Now bring to simmer and add wine and cook for 5 minutes or until the wine reduces to half.
- Add thyme and heavy cream.
- Slow down the heat further and let it boil.
- Now add the cooked chicken to the wok and cook in slow flame for about four minutes.
- Garnish with nicely chopped parsley and serve.

Nutritional value:

Calories: 276 | Carbohydrate: 6g | Protein: 25g | Fat: 10g |Cholesterol: 85mg | Sodium: 151mg | Potassium: 520mg | Sugars: 2g

8. HOLY YUM CHICKEN -US STYLE

Preparation: 5 minutes | Cooking: 40 minutes | Servings: 4

Ingredients:

- Boneless chicken thighs (skinless) – 2 pounds
- Dijon Mustard – ½ cup
- Pure maple syrup – ¼ cup
- Rice wine – 1 tablespoon
- Salt – as required
- Ground black pepper – ¼ teaspoon
- Cornstarch – 1 tablespoon
- Rosemary (fresh) – 2 teaspoons for garnishing

Cooking directions:

- Heat the oven to 450 degrees.
- Take an oven safe pan and line with aluminum foil.

- Mix Dijon mustard, maple syrup, rice wine vinegar and seasonings in a small pan.
- Place the chicken in the foil and pour the mix over the chicken.
- Roll the chicken in the mix and let it coat evenly on it.
- Bake it open for 40 minutes.
- Take out the chicken and let it cool for 5 minutes.
- Keep the liquid and add a teaspoon of cornstarch and slightly heat up.
- Make sure the liquid thickens and if not add little more cornstarch.
- Pour the liquid over the chicken.
- Dust rosemary on top at the time of serving.

Approximate Nutritional values:

Calories: 327 | Carbohydrate: 16g | Protein: 24g | Fat: 20g |Sugars: 14g | Cholesterol: 113g | Sodium: 2589mg

9. CHICKEN RICE – ASIAN STYLE

Preparation: 10 minutes | Cooking: 20 minutes | Servings: 6

Ingredients:

- Olive oil – 3 tablespoons
- Chopped onion – 1 large
- Chicken thighs (boneless, skinless) – 2 pounds
- Rice – 1½ cups
- Seasonings
- Chicken broth – 2 cups
- Rice wine – ½ cup
- Saffron – 1 Pinch
- Chopped Parsley – ½ bunches
- Salt – to taste
- Pepper – as required

Cooking directions:

- Take a cast iron pan and bring to heat.
- Pour oil and add onion when the oil becomes hot.
- Cook it until the onions become soft.
- Now put the chicken into the pan and cook it until it becomes brown.
- Remove the chicken to a plate and keep the onion in the pan.
- Add the rice in that pan and stir it carefully.
- Add the chicken again in the pan and sprinkle salt and pepper as required.
- Now pour rice wine, chicken broth, and water over the rice and chicken.
- Dust in saffron.
- Cover the lid and cook on low heat for about 20-30 minutes or until the rice is cooked well.
- After 20-25 minutes, open the lid and check the water content in the rice and make sure there is no water before you stop cooking.
- Sprinkle with fresh parsley and serve.

Nutritional value:

Calories: 589 | Carbohydrate: 39g | Protein: 28g | Fat: 32g | Cholesterol: 148mg | Sodium: 408mg | Potassium: 466mg

10. CASHEW CHICKEN – US STYLE

Preparation: 10 minutes | Cooking: 4 hours| Servings: 4

Cooking directions:

- Olive oil – 1 tablespoon
- Skinless chicken thighs with bone - 2 ½ lbs.
- Sea Salt – 1 teaspoon
- Ground black pepper – ½ teaspoon
- Soy Sauce (low sodium) – ½ cup
- Rice wine – ¼ cup
- Chili paste – 1 teaspoon
- Raw honey – 1 tablespoon
- Minced garlic – 3 cloves
- Minced ginger - 1 teaspoon
- Cashews – 1 cup
- Sliced green onions – 4

- Cooked brown rice – as required for serving.

Cooking directions:

- First of all, season the chicken with pepper and salt.
- In a pan, heat oil and put chicken
- Cook it for 2 minutes until the chicken becomes brown on both sides by flipping sides.
- Put the chicken into a slow cooker bowl.
- Mix soy sauce, rice wine vinegar, and ginger, cashews along with honey, garlic and chili paste in a medium bowl.
- Pour the mix over the chicken.
- Close the slow cooker and cook at low temperature for 3-4 hours.
- Dress it with sliced onion on top.
- Serve hot along with boiled/steamed rice.

Nutritional value:

Calories: 518 | Carbohydrate: 3.1g | Protein: 42.9g | Fat: 36.9g |Cholesterol: 218.1mg | Sodium: 990.1mg | Sugars: 0.2g | Fiber: 3.6g

ASIAN MEAT MEALS

1. CHINESE ORANGE BEEF

Preparation – 10 minutes, Cooking – 15 minutes,
Serves – 4 servings

Ingredients:

- Vegetable oil – 3 tablespoons
- Rice wine – 1 tablespoon
- Chopped beef steak – 1¼ pound
- Cornstarch – 2 tablespoons
- Orange juice – 2 big oranges

- Orange zest – half of the orange
- Caster sugar – 3 tablespoons
- Soya sauce (gluten free) – 5 tablespoons
- Garlic mashed – 2 or 3 cloves
- Ginger finely chopped – 1 tablespoon
- Rep pepper finely sliced – 1 or 2
- Sliced onion chunks – 1 large
- Pepper - as required
- Salt - to taste

For serving:

- Boiled rice
- Spring onion (diagonally chopped) 4

Cooking directions:

- Heat a non-stick frying pan and pour oil into it.
- With the help of a kitchen paper towel, pat the beef dry and toss it with some corn flour, black pepper, and salt.
- When the beef is completely coated with the mixture, deep fry it until it becomes crispy and crunchy.
- Remove the fried beef onto a plate and keep aside and discard the oil.
- In a bowl, mix sugar, zest, orange juice, soya sauce, ginger, garlic, and rice wine. Keep it aside.
- In the same pan which had been used for cooking the beef, pour some oil and add sliced onion and chopped red bell pepper.
- Fry it for just 5 minutes but keep it still raw and crunchy.
- Put the fried veggies in the orange sauce and also the fried beef.
- Stir it for 1 minute or so.
- Add some cornflour mixed with water to thicken the consistency, if required.

- Garnish with scallions or spring onions and serve with boiled rice.

Approximate Nutritional Values:

Calories: 349 | Cholesterol: 73mg |Protein: 31g | Fat: 14g |Sodium: 1332mg |Potassium: 686mg |Carbohydrates: 22g | Dietary Fiber: 1g | Sugars: 14g

2. Pepper Steak – Chinese Style

Preparation: 5 minutes | Cooking: 10 minutes | Servings: 4

Ingredients:

- Top Beef – Nicely trimmed 12 ounces
- Soy sauce - 4 teaspoons and 3 tablespoons
- Rice wine – 1 tablespoon
- Onion finely chopped in long strips – 1 big
- Cornstarch – 3 tablespoons
- Vegetable oil – 1 tablespoon
- Bell pepper (finely long sliced) – 1 big
- Black pepper – ½ teaspoon
- Red pepper (partially crushed) - ¼ teaspoon

Preparation:

- Chop the beef into thin slices.

- Put the beef slices in a bowl and pour 4 teaspoons of soy sauce and stir.
- Now pour 1 tablespoon cornstarch and stir.
- Add 1 tablespoon of rice wine and combine.
- Add some black pepper as required.
- Take a separate bowl and mix 2 tablespoons of cornstarch, 2 tablespoons of water and 3 teaspoons of soy sauce.
- Heat a pan on medium-high temperature and pour some oil in it.
- When the oil becomes hot, place the beef in the pan and let it cook for 30 seconds until it becomes brown.
- Stir the meat occasionally and continue cooking for about 3 minutes.
- Once all sides become brown, remove it to a plate.
- In the same pan pour a little oil and heat on medium-high temperature.
- When the oil becomes hot add some finely sliced and chopped onions and peppers.
- Let them cook for 3-4 minutes while continuing to stir. Keep it a little raw and crispy.
- Now add the cooked beef to the pan again and keep the temperature low-medium.
- Add some sauce and finely crushed red flakes.
- Pour cornstarch mixture and continue heating for 2 minutes. When the liquid becomes thick, stop heating.
- Serve hot, delicious Pepper Steak.

Nutritional Value:

Calories: 187 | Fat: 6g | Protein: 22g | Carbohydrate: 12g | Sugar: 3g |Cholesterol: 54mg |Sodium: 668mg | Fiber: 2g | Sugars: 3g

3. MONGOLIAN BEEF

Preparation: 10 minutes | Cooking: 20 minutes | Servings: 4

Ingredients:

- Flank steak - 1½ pounds
- Rice wine - 1 tablespoon
- Cornstarch - 1 tablespoon
- Olive oil - 1 tablespoon
- Brown sugar - ½ cup
- Garlic (finely chopped & mashed) - 10 cloves
- Fresh ginger paste - 1 tablespoon
- Soy sauce - ½ cup
- Water - 1 cup
- Red pepper flakes - 1 teaspoon
- Green onions (fine strips) – for garnish
- Sesame seeds – For garnish

Cornstarch puree:

- Cornstarch – 2 tablespoons
- Water – ½ cup preferred

Cooking Directions:

- Take your electric pressure cooker and heat it. Press the sauté button and then click on adjust and select 'More,' so that food will be sautéed more.
- In a zip lock bag add the slices of beef and some cornstarch. Shake it nicely so that it gets an even coating.
- Pour some oil and add beef slices coated with cornstarch in the pressure cooker. Sauté it for some time.
- Let the beef turn a little brown and add water if needed to scrape the beef that has stuck in the cooker.
- Now add the finely crushed and minced garlic and ginger with soy sauce, rice wine, brown sugar, and water.
- Add some red pepper flakes according to spiciness.
- Swirl everything so that all ingredients can mix and coat nicely.
- Now close the cooker and let it cook on high pressure for 7-8 minutes. After that let it cook on a natural mode for 10 more minutes.
- Make cornstarch paste in between by mixing cornstarch with water and ensuring that there are no lumps.
- Add the paste and cook it for another 4 minutes on Sauté mode.
- Let the paste settle for some minutes.
- Serve the dish in the plate.
- Garnish with spring onions and sesame seeds.

Nutritional Value:

Calories: 292 | Carbohydrate: 28g | Sugar: 21g | Protein: 22g |Fat: 9g |Cholesterol: 54mg | Sodium: 1362mg | Sugars: 21g |Potassium: 409mg

4. Chinese Broccoli Beef

Preparation: 10 minutes | Cooking: 10 minutes | Servings: 4

Ingredients:

- Beefsteak - ½ pound
- Soy sauce - 1½ teaspoon
- Cornstarch - 1 teaspoon
- Black pepper (freshly ground) - 1 teaspoon
- Broccoli florets (chopped) - 1 pound
- Cooking oil - 1 tablespoon
- Garlic (finely chopped) - 2 cloves
- Fresh ginger (finely grated) - 1 teaspoon

Ingredients for Stir Fry Sauce:

- Oyster sauce - 3 tablespoons
- Chinese rice wine - 2 teaspoons

- Chinese black vinegar - 2 teaspoons (young balsamic vinegar)

Cooking Directions:

- Take beef steak and slice it into long thin pieces across the grain.
- In a medium bowl place the beef. Now add and combine the rest of the ingredients like soy sauce, freshly ground black pepper and cornstarch. Place the mixture aside for 10 minutes to marinate.
- In a separate bowl put the ingredients of the Stir Fry Sauce and mix them as per the quantities mentioned above.
- Now, in a pan add 1 cup of water and then add chopped broccoli when the water starts to boil. Let it sit on steam for 3-4 minutes until the broccoli becomes soft yet still with bite.
- Once the broccoli is cooked well, drain out the water and heat the pan so that it becomes dry and then add some cooking oil in it.
- When the oil starts heating, add the marinated beef mixture in it and cook it for 3-4 minutes. Stir the mixture in between. Let the beef become brownish and crispy. Flip the beef in between to ensure it gets evenly cooked.
- Now move the beef to a corner of the pan and add finely chopped and minced ginger-garlic on the other side. Let it fry for 20 seconds and then mix everything well.
- Take the entire mixture out for some time and pour the Stir-Fry sauce in the same pan. Continue heating for about 20 seconds so that it becomes thick. Now add the cooked broccoli in the sauce and toss everything well.
- Transfer the food to a serving bowl.
- Serve it hot.

Approximate Nutritional Values:

Calories: 162 | Protein: 15 | Carbohydrates: 10g | Fat: 6g |Cholesterol: 34mg | Sodium: 562mg | Potassium: 551mg | Dietary fiber: 2g | Sugars: 1g

5. CHINESE BEEF FRIED RICE

Preparation: 20 minutes | Cooking: 15 minutes | Servings: 4-6

Ingredients:

For the beef:

- Flank steak (diced to small cubes): 10 ounces
- Salt - ¼ teaspoon
- Water – 2 or 3 tablespoons
- Baking soda – Just a pinch
- Soy sauce (mushroom flavor) - 1 teaspoon
- Cornstarch - 1 teaspoon
- Cooking oil – 1 or 2 teaspoons

For the rest of the dish:

- Shaoxing wine – 2 tablespoons
- Hot water – 1 or 2 tablespoons
- Sugar - ¼ teaspoon

- Sesame oil - ½ teaspoon
- Soy sauce - 1½ tablespoon
- Dark soy sauce - 2 teaspoons
- MSG - ½ teaspoon
- White pepper grounded (fresh) - 1 teaspoon
- Rice cooked - 5 cups
- Canola oil - 3 tablespoons
- Eggs (beaten) – 2
- Onion, chopped to chunks - 1 medium size
- Peas - ¾ cup
- Scallion, finely chopped – 1

Cooking Directions:

- Take a medium bowl and put beef into it.
- Add cornstarch, dark soy sauce, water, salt, and baking soda into the bowl.
- Toss the mixture and keep it aside to marinate for about 10-15 minutes.
- In a separate small bowl add sugar, sesame oil, soy sauces, white pepper, hot water, and MSG. This mixture is the sauce for fried rice.
- Toss your cooked rice nicely with your hands or fork as per your convenience.
- Heat a pan and let it become hot.
- Now add some cooking oil and when the oil becomes hot add the beaten eggs into it. Start scraping the eggs so that they cook well. Take it out in a bowl when cooked.
- Heat the pan again and pour oil in it. When the oil becomes hot, put the marinated mixture and let it cook for 25 seconds. Stir the beef and let it fry for some time. When the meat becomes brown transfer it to a bowl.
- Again, in the same pan add some oil and fry the sliced onions. Let the onions turn crisp and brown. At this

junction, you can put the rice. If the rice is taken out from the refrigerator, then toss it with few drops of water.

- After the rice is sautéed for 2 minutes add the sauce. Stir everything well so that sauce will mix with the dish thoroughly.
- Further, add beef and extra juices (if any).
- Now add eggs into the dish and swirl to break large lumps. Let it cook for about 30 seconds. Now, with the help of spatula shove the rice in the middle of the pan to heat the out circle nicely.
- Pour the Shaoxing wine on the space created and let it cook for another 20 seconds.
- Serve the hot and delicious dish with chili oil.

Nutritional Value:

Calories: 337 | Fat: 19g | Cholesterol: 111mg | Sodium: 345mg | Potassium: 262mg | Carbohydrates: 25g | Dietary fiber: 0.9g | Sugars: 1g | Protein: 16g

6. Korean Beef

Preparation: 10 minutes | Cooking: 15 minutes | Servings: 6

Ingredients:

- Beef, boneless, diced to cubes – 3 pounds
- Beef broth - ½ cup
- Soy sauce (low sodium) – ⅓ cup (less sodium)
- Rice wine - 1 tablespoon
- Brown sugar - ⅓ cup
- Garlic, finely chopped - 4 cloves
- Sesame oil - 1 tablespoon
- Ginger, finely chopped) - 1 tablespoon
- Sriracha - 1 teaspoon
- Onion powder - ½ teaspoon
- White pepper - ½ teaspoon
- Cornstarch - 3 tablespoons
- Sesame seeds - 1 teaspoon
- Green onions, finely wedged to slices – 2 large

Cooking Directions:

- Take a big bowl and add beef broth, garlic, sesame oil, and rice wine, brown sugar, soy sauce, Sriracha, white pepper, and some onion powder. Combine the ingredients altogether.
- In a cooker (Electric One) add the beef and beef broth mixture. Combine all the things well.
- After tossing everything set the cooking timer to 15 minutes and set to high-pressure cooking.
- After 15 minutes of cooking let the pressure release naturally.
- For cornstarch puree, take a small bowl and mix cornstarch with water and mix so that there are no lumps.
- Now adjust the setting to high sauté and gradually stir the cornstarch puree and stir it continuously to avoid lumps.
- Let it cook for 2-3 minutes so that the sauce thickens.
- For mouth-watering presentation and taste, garnish with green onions and sesame seeds.

Nutritional Value:

Calories: 460.2 | Fat: 26.9g | Protein: 21.7g | Carbohydrate: 42.1g |Dietary fiber: 0.9g |Cholesterol: 85.1mg |Sodium: 898.3mg | Potassium: 498.8mg | Sugars: 37.0g

7. JAPANESE BEEF BOWL

Preparation: 5 minutes | Cooking: 15 minutes | Servings: 2

Ingredients:

- Beef (chopped into thin slices) - ¾ pound
- Scallion or Green Onion - 1
- Rice wine: 2 tablespoons
- Sake – 1 tablespoon
- Onion chopped – ½ large
- Dashi - ½ cup
- Sugar - 1 tablespoon
- Soy sauce - 2 tablespoons
- Red ginger (pickled) – 2 tablespoons
- Onsen Tamago (optional) – 2 or 3

Cooking Directions:

- Clean and wash the sliced beef and pat ready for cooking.

- On a chopping tray, slice the onion into long thin slices. Side by side, chop the green onions as well.
- Take a frying pan and heat it on medium high temperature.
- Add dashi, sake, mirin, sugar and the required amount of soy sauce. (Quantities as mentioned above).
- Cover the pan and let the sauce cook for some time.
- Now, add onions in the sauce and spread it all over.
- Once again cover the lid so that the sauce doesn't evaporate.
- Have a look at onions and make sure they are nice crispy.
- Now add the beef and let it cook.
- Let the pink color of the beef disappear and remove the foam using a sieve.
- After cooking over, serve them immediately with steamed rice.
- Garnish with spring onions, pickled red ginger and Onsen Tamago

Nutritional Value:

Calories: 730 | Fat: 27g | Protein: 30g |Cholesterol: 70mg | Sodium: 1310mg | Carbohydrates: 91g |Dietary fiber: 3g |Sugars: 5g

8. KOREAN BEEF BIBIMBAP

Preparation: 10 minutes | Cooking: 20 minutes | Servings: 2

Ingredients:

- Ground beef - ¾ pound
- Rice wine – 5 tablespoons
- Jasmine rice - ¾ cup
- Zucchini – 1
- Button Mushrooms – 4 ounces
- Scallions – 2 units
- Carrot – 1
- Ginger fresh grated – 1 tablespoon
- Garlic, minced – 2 cloves
- Sesame oil – 1 teaspoon
- Sriracha – 1 tablespoon

- Soy sauce – 3 tablespoons
- Vegetable oil – 4 teaspoons
- Pepper fresh, ground – 1 teaspoon
- Salt – as per taste
- Sugar – 1 ½ tablespoon

Cooking Directions:

- First, let us prepare all the vegetables. Chop zucchini into a thin semicircle, cut mushrooms, and scallions. Chop the ginger and garlic and mince them nicely. Peel the carrot and chop it into thin slices.
- Boil some water in a large bowl and put little salt as per taste.
- Now put the rice and cook it for 15 minutes on medium heat.
- Take a small bowl and add white scallion, salt as per taste and rice wine. Toss them nicely and keep aside.
- Now in a separate bowl, add sesame oil, 2 teaspoons Sriracha, 1½ tablespoons sugar and 1 ½ tablespoon soy sauce. Stir them for a minute or so and keep it aside.
- Take a pan and heat it on a medium flame.
- Put in some carrots and add salt and pepper.
- Cook for about 3-4 minutes until they become crispy. Take them out of the pan and heat it again with some oil.
- Now fry zucchini for some time and set it aside.
- In the same pan drizzle some oil and cook mushrooms. Add salt and pepper and set it aside after the cooking is over.
- Now, in a pan take some oil and heat on medium low temperature.
- When the oil becomes hot add minced ginger and garlic.
- Cook it for about 30 seconds.
- Add beef and toss it well until it changes the color from pink to brown.

- Add remaining soy sauce to the beef and cook it for about 3 more minutes.
- In a serving bowl, serve beef first. After that serve all the fried vegetables for a delicious and eye-catching look.
- Drizzle some sauce over it.
- Garnish it with scallions green and pepper.

Nutritional Value:

Calories: 760 | Fat: 33g | Carbohydrate: 78g | Protein: 37g |Cholesterol: 95mg | Sodium: 1100mg |Dietary fiber: 5g |Sugars: 11g

9. AMERICAN LAMB SHANKS

Preparation: 15 minutes | Cooking: 3 hours | Servings: 4

Ingredients:

- Olive oil – 3 or 4 tablespoons
- White rice wine – 1 cup
- Lamb shanks - 4
- Lamb stock – 4 cups
- Chopped celery stalks - 2
- Onions, diced to chunks - 1 big size
- Carrots, chopped - 2
- Garlic, minced - 6 cloves
- Anchovy paste - 1 teaspoon
- Ground cinnamon - 2 teaspoon
- Bay leaves - 2 large
- Juniper berries - 6
- Tomato paste/puree - 2 tablespoon

- All-purpose flour - 3 tablespoons
- Pepper – as required
- Salt – to taste
- Fresh parsley – finely chopped into pieces

Cooking Directions:

- Preheat the cooker on low-medium heat.
- In a separate pot, add some oil and let it become hot. When the oil becomes hot add lamb in it. Sprinkle salt and pepper as required.
- Now transfer the lamb into the cooker.
- Add all the vegetables in the lamb mixture and sauté it for 3-5 minutes. Let it turn soft.
- Once the vegetables are sautéed, add tomato puree and anchovy paste.
- After that, add the spices like cinnamon, salt as per taste, juniper berries and pepper (as per taste).
- Drizzle flour so that the vegetables get a nice coating.
- Once vegetables had a good coating, add rice wine and stock. Let it boil for 3-4 minutes so that the sauce thickens.
- Set the cooker to slow mode and add the vegetable sauce mixture to the lamb.
- Let it cook for 3-8 hours in a slow cooker.

Nutritional Value:

Calories: 455 | Fat: 17g | Protein: 45g | Carbohydrates: 17g |Cholesterol: 128mg | Dietary fiber: 2g | Sugars: 4g |Protein: 45g | Sodium: 632mg |Potassium: 726mg

10. Peruvian Lomo

Preparation: 30 minutes | Cooking: 20 minutes | Servings: 4

Ingredients:

- Beef, ¼" sliced chunks – 1 pound
- French fries (frozen) - 16 ounces
- Rice wine: ¼ cup
- Vegetable oil – as per requirements
- Onion, strip cuts – 1 big size
- Tomatoes, sliced in large strips – 3 large
- Yellow chili pepper – 1
- Soy sauce – as per taste
- Salt – to taste
- Pepper – as required

- Finely chopped fresh parsley – 2 tablespoons (for garnishing)

Cooking Directions:

- Start with the frozen French fries. Cook them as per the instructions on the package.
- While, French fries are cooking, heat a nonstick pan on medium heat and pour some oil in it.
- When the oil becomes hot, add the meat.
- Add salt and pepper as per the taste.
- Let the meat fry for a couple of minutes. After it start to release some juice take it out from the pan and keep aside.
- In the same pan add some more oil and sauté the onions until they become pale and translucent.
- Now, add tomato and mash it a bit so that it softens.
- Add some soy sauce and rice wine in the mixture and let it cook for few seconds.
- At this point, add the French fries and cover the pan with a lid and cook about 4 minutes, so that the beef can cook nicely.
- Place the food onto a serving dish.
- Sprinkle salt and pepper as per your taste.
- Garnish the lip-smacking recipe with some chopped parsley.

Nutritional Value:

Calories: 498 | Fat: 27.3g | Protein: 26.3g | Carbohydrates: 37.8g | Cholesterol: 74mg| Sodium: 606mg | Potassium: 1250mg | Dietary fiber: 4.6g | Sugars: 6g

Asian Fish Meals

1. Steamed Fish -Chinese Style

Preparation: 10 minutes | Cooking: 25 minutes | Servings: 4

Ingredients:

- Rice wine – 2 cups
- Fish fillets (fresh) – 1 pound
- Light soya sauce –2 tablespoons
- Honey – 1 tablespoon
- Water – $^2/_3$ cup
- White pepper – 1 teaspoon
- Sugar – 2 teaspoons
- Cornstarch (mixed with 2 teaspoon water) -2 teaspoons
- Cold water-2 teaspoons

- Toasted sesame oil- 2 teaspoons
- Green onions (finely chopped) - 3 tablespoons
- Salt – to taste

Cooking directions:

- Arrange all the ingredients and keep them in a place so that it will be easy to cook.
- Take 2 cups of rice wine, water, soya sauce, sugar, white pepper, 1 teaspoon salt, in a non-stick pan and boil it.
- Boil the prepared liquid and add corn-starch mixture to it. Cook for 30 seconds and let the quantity reduce to half and liquid become thick. Once done, keep it aside.
- While the cooking continues, you can marinate the fish fillets with salt and toasted sesame oil and set it aside.
- Now put the fish fillets in the prepared liquid and cook it on a low heat for 2 minutes.
- After that take it out from the heat and keep it for cooling for 5 minutes in a covered container.
- Your fish fillet is ready to serve.
- Transfer it to a serving plate.
- Drizzle with sauce and garnish with green onions.

Approximate Nutritional values:

Calories: 316.7 | Carbohydrate: 10.4g | Protein: 27.6g | Sugars: 2.4g | Fat: 3.3g | Cholesterol: 62.3 mg | Sodium: 1758.4mg | Dietary fiber: 0.4g

2. STEAMED WHOLE FISH – VIETNAMESE STYLE

Preparation: 5 minutes | Cooking: 25 minutes | Servings: 4

Ingredients:

- Whitefish (Whole with head and tail) - 1½ pound
- Light soya sauce – ¼ cup
- Rice wine – 1 tablespoon
- Scallion (light green parts julienned) -1
- Cilantro springs-4
- Canola oil – ½ cup
- Fresh ginger (finely julienned)– 2 pieces
- Black pepper (ground) – as required
- Kosher salt – to taste

Cooking directions:

- First, rinse the fish in cold water and dry it with paper towels.

- After cleaning, season the fish both outer and inner area with salt and pepper.
- Place the fish in a large ovenproof plate.
- Pour half of the ginger in the mouth of the fish and reaming should be spread on top of the fish.
- Pour water in a large wok for steaming.
- Boil the water over high heat.
- Once the water boils and starts to steam, place the plate containing fish for steaming.
- Cover it and steam for at least 8 minutes.
- Steam the fish until the fish flesh is easy to remove with a knife.
- While steaming continues, start mixing rice wine, sauce, and 1 tablespoon of water, in a small bowl and keep it aside.
- After steaming is over, remove the fish and plate from the steamer.
- Now spread scallion and cilantro over the fish.
- Take, a small sauté pan, pour some oil and heat at high temperature. It should not smoke.
- Pour the hot oil on scallion and cilantro so that it can cook.
- Now the fish is ready to serve.
- Drizzle the prepared sauce mixture on the top of the fish and serve it hot.

Approximate Nutritional value:

Calories: 428 | Carbohydrate: 3 g | Protein: 36g | Sugars: 1.4g | Fat: 30g | Fiber: 1g | Cholesterol: 85mg

3. Asian Style Steamed Snapper

Preparation: 15 minutes | Cooking: 15 minutes | Servings: 4

Ingredients:

- Whole snapper with head and tail (scaled) - 1¾ pounds
- Peanut oil-3 teaspoons
- Chinese rice wine – 2 tablespoons
- Green shallots (sliced diagonally and end trimmed) -4
- Ginger fresh (finely shredded)-2 tablespoons
- Red chili julienned – 1
- Coriander leaves, fresh - ¼ cup
- Light soya sauce – 1½ tablespoons
- Sugar – a small pinch
- Sesame oil - ½ teaspoon
- Steamed rice to serve

Cooking directions:

- Pour some water into the wok and make it ready for steaming
- Place a steaming rack over the wok.
- Mix red chili, ginger, green shallot in a bowl. After that take a large plate and sprinkle the ⅓rd part of shallot mixture in the heatproof plate.
- Keep the fish over the plate.
- Pour the half of the remaining shallot mixture into the fish mouth. Then remaining shallot mixture should be sprinkled on the top of the fish.
- Take a small bowl and mix the rice wine, soya sauce, sugar, and sesame oil.
- Pour this mixture over the fish.
- Place the heatproof plate in the steaming rack carefully.
- Boil the water in the wok and after boiling reduce the heat to medium and continue the steaming process.
- After steaming the fish for 12-15 minutes and when the fish cooked well, stop steaming. Check the fish with a knife or sharp folk for estimating the cooking status.
- Remove the fish to a serving plate and dash the coriander leaves over the fish.
- Take a sauté pan and heat the peanut oil.
- Stop before smoking and drizzle the hot oil over fish.
- Fish is ready to serve.

Nutritional value:

Calories: 850 | Carbohydrate: 9g | Protein: 27 g | Sugars: 1g | Fat: 6g |Cholesterol:77 mg| Fiber: 1g |Sodium: 627.78mg

4. Chinese Steamed Fish

Preparation: 15 minutes | Cooking: 15 minutes | Servings: 2

Ingredients:

- Dried chili peppers – 2
- Tilapia or flounder with head and tail, scaled and gutted - 1¼ pound
- Shaoxing wine - 2 tablespoons
- Sichuan peppercorn- ½ teaspoon
- Seasoned soya sauce for seafood- 2 tablespoons
- Peanut oil/vegetable oil- 1 tablespoon
- Sesame oil- 1 tablespoon
- Green onion (chopped into strips) - 1 cup
- Ginger (julienned) – 1 thumb size

Cooking directions:

- Wash the fish thoroughly and drain.
- Keep the fish in a mesh colander for 30 minutes. Let it dry completely.
- Place a quarter of the green onions in an oven-safe plate so that it could accommodate the fish. The green onion should be appropriately spread on the plate so that that fish can place over it and it will not stick on the plate while cooking.
- Next, stuff the fish cavity with fresh ginger slices, and green onion.
- Rub both sides of the fish with sesame oil. Cover the fish with a quarter part of the remaining green onion.
- Pour Shaoxing wine over the fish.
- Make the vessel ready for the steaming process. Take a wok and pour a ½ inch of water in it and mount a steaming rack in the wok.
- Keep the plate containing fish over the steam rack and boil the water.
- Cover the plate and let cook in the steam for about 8 minutes. Steam the fish until it becomes ready. Use a knife or fork to check the cooking status of the fish by pulling the flesh.
- Once fish is ready carefully transfer the fish to a plate. You can use a spatula to transfer the fish. Take a chopstick to remove onion and ginger from inside the fish and then discard it.
- After removing the used ginger and onion keep the remaining ginger slice and onion over the top of fish and keep it aside. Make ready the seasoned soy sauce for the further cooking process.
- Take a wok or non-stick sauté pan and heat the oil.

- Once the oil becomes hot, break chili, pepper and Sichuan corn into it. Stir this mixture with a spatula for around 40 secs so that it can be ready to sprinkle. Discard the chili, pepper and Sichuan corn.
- Drizzle the hot oil over the fish with the help of a spoon. When you drizzle oil over the fish, you can hear the sizzling sound when the hot oil touches the fish. Then pour the seasoned soya sauce over the fish.
- Serve hot.

Approximate Nutritional values:

Calories: 353 | Carbohydrate: 5.5 g | Protein: 47.9 g | Sugars: 2.4g | Fat: 14.7g | Cholesterol: 99 mg | Sodium: 625mg | Potassium: 184mg | Dietary fiber: 1.6g

5. Korean Fish Stir-Fry

Preparation: 20 minutes | Cooking: 10 minutes | Servings: 4

Ingredients:

- Ling fillets - 1½ pound
- Rice stick noodles- 6½ ounce
- Rice bran or sunflower oil-2 teaspoon
- Spring onion, finely chopped - 4
- Green capsicum thinly sliced - 2
- Red capsicum, julienned - 1
- Watercress springs- 2 cups

Marinade ingredients

- Chinese rice wine – 1 tablespoon
- Garlic crushed – 2 cloves
- Chili powder- ½ teaspoon
- Soya sauce - 2 tablespoons

- Sesame seeds toasted- 2 teaspoons
- Sesame oil - 2 teaspoons

Cooking directions:

- Take a medium bowl and add all ingredients of marinade and combine it.
- Put fish into the marinade and turn it to coat. Keep it marinating for 10 minutes.
- Cook the noodles as mentioned on the packet and drain them.
- Take a wok and heat some oil in it on high temperature.
- Add the marinated fish into it. Fry it by slowly stirring the mixture for 1 min. Do not crush the fish. Reserve the marinade mix.
- Add onion and capsicum and stir fry it for 2 minutes.
- After that add the marinated mix into it and cook for 2-3 minutes until the fish is cooked thoroughly and the sauce starts to melt over it.
- After performing the above steps, stop cooking and fold in the watercress.
- Serve the fish over the noodles.

Nutritional value:

Calories: 253 | Carbohydrate: 6 g | Protein: 37.9 g | Sugars: 3 g | Fat: 14.7g| Cholesterol: 87 mg

6. Halibut – Asian Style

Preparation: 20 minutes | Cooking: 40 minutes | Servings: 4

Ingredients:

- Fillets halibut – 6 (4 ounces)
- Vegetable oil- 1 teaspoon
- Shallots -1 finely chopped
- Rice vinegar - 1 tablespoon
- Japanese sweet wine (mirin) - ½ cup
- Garlic finely chopped – 2 cloves
- Black bean sauce – 1 tablespoon
- Soya sauce – 1 tablespoon
- Sesame oil – 1 teaspoon
- Pepper - ¼ teaspoon

- Fresh cilantro chopped - 2 tablespoons

Cooking directions:

- In a nonstick pan, heat oil at medium-low temperature.
- When the oil becomes hot, put chopped garlic and shallot and sauté until its fragrance emanates.
- Now, put black bean sauce, soya sauce and rice wine in it and stir properly.
- Continue stirring until it boils, and the quantity reduces to half and the consistency thickens.
- Once the liquid becomes half, stop heating and add rice vinegar and keep it aside.
- Wash fish and pat it dry with the help of a paper towel.
- After that add sesame oil and sprinkle pepper on fish.
- Slightly pat oil on the grill and preheat it on high temperature.
- Put the fish on the grill and sear each side for 5 minutes, or you can grill it until it is cooked well.
- Once cooking is over move to a serving plate.
- Garnish with cilantro and drizzle sauce on the top of the fish.
- Serve hot.

Nutritional value:

Calories: 194 | Carbohydrate: 8.6 g | Protein: 23.9 g | Sugars: 3 g | Fat: 4.3g|Cholesterol: 36 mg |Sugars: 7g | Potassium: 552mg | Sodium: 231mg

7. Rice Wine Glazed Salmon-Japanese Style

Preparation: 10 minutes | Cooking: 10 minutes | Servings: 4

Ingredients:

- Salmon fillets (skin removed) – 4 (6 ounces)
- Water – ½ cup
- Japanese sweet rice wine (mirin) - ¼ cup
- Light brown sugar (use only light brown sugar) – ¼ cup
- Soya sauce (gluten-free) – ¼ cup
- Rice vinegar- 1 tablespoon
- Scallion julienned – 2

Cooking directions:

- Take a shallow dish which can hold at least 4 salmon fillets.

- Add mirin, brown sugar and soya sauce in the shallow dish.
- Stir until sugar dissolves and add salmon in this dish and leave it to marinate for 5 -10 minutes. Flip it once so that it can have even coating.
- Take a large skillet and heat it in low-medium temperature.
- Put salmon fillets in the hot, dry pan and cook them until they get a dark brown glazed coating. Pay attention while dry frying it and never allow it to spoil. Flip the fillets over so that both sides will get an even frying.
- Once frying is over, reduce the heat to medium and add the marinade and water in the pan.
- Cook it for 3-5 minutes so that it becomes ready to eat. Add a little water to maintain the consistency if required. Do not let it burn because if it burns it will taste bad.
- When the sauce becomes hot and starts to bubble turn off the heat.
- Transfer salmon fillets onto the serving plate leaving the sauce in the pan.
- Now add rice vinegar in the sauce and stir it properly and heat on low temperature.
- Once it starts to bubble, stop heating and pour the sauce over the salmon fillets.
- Garnish with scallions and serve hot.

Nutritional value:

Calories: 437 | Carbohydrate: 16 g | Protein: 36 g | Sugars: 314g | Fat: 23g|Cholesterol: 94 mg |Protein: 36g | Sodium: 1005mg | Fiber: 0g

8. Chinese Ginger Scallion Fish

Preparation: 10 minutes | Cooking: 10 minutes | Servings: 4

Ingredients:

Mix and marinate section:

- Whitefish (Tilapia) - 1 pound
- Soya sauce – 3 tablespoons
- Rice wine – 2 tablespoons
- Chinese black bean paste -1 tablespoon
- Minced ginger - 1 teaspoon
- Garlic minced – 1 teaspoon

Vegetable section

- Peanut oil – 1 tablespoon
- Julienned ginger – 2 tablespoons
- Julienned green onion - ¼ cup

- Chopped cilantro - ¼ cup

Cooking directions:

- Keep fish pieces on a plate and mix the ingredients for the sauce.
- Pour this sauce over fish and marinate it thoroughly and keep it aside for 20 to 30 minutes.
- Now chop the vegetables and keep them aside.
- Use an instant pot for steaming.
- Pour water in the inner liner and make it ready for steaming.
- Set the cooker on steam mode.
- Place the fish in the steam basket and steam for 2 minutes on a low heat, reserving the marinade mix.
- After 2 minutes of steaming quickly release the pressure.
- Take a sauté pan and add some oil.
- Heat it on low, medium temperature.
- Once the oil becomes hot, slow down the temperature and add minced ginger.
- Cook for 10 seconds.
- After that add scallions and cilantro and stir it. Scallions and cilantro will get soft after cooking for 2 minutes.
- Once it becomes soft, add the reserved marinade and cook it thoroughly until the sauce becomes thick.
- When the cause become thick, stop cooking and pour it over the fish.
- Serve hot.

Nutritional value:

Calories: 171 kcal | Carbohydrate: 4 g | Protein: 24g | Sugars: 1 g | Fat: 5g

9. Fish with Soft Tofu and Black Beans

Preparation: 10 minutes | Cooking: 20 minutes | Servings: 4

Ingredients:

- Skinned halibut/ salmon fillet (cut into ½" thick) - 1 pound
- Shaoxing rice wine -1 tablespoon
- Water-packed soft tofu- 1 package (18 oz.)
- Chinese black bean garlic sauce- 1 tablespoon
- Sesame oil – 1 tablespoon
- Soya sauce – 2 teaspoons
- Dark soya sauce – 2 teaspoons
- Minced garlic - 1 teaspoon
- Sugar – ¼ teaspoon

- Fresh ginger julienned - 1 tablespoon
- Green onions (1" cut size) - 1 large

Cooking directions:

- First, make the marinade. Mix black bean garlic sauce, Shaoxing rice wine, sesame oil, soya sauce, dark soya sauce, garlic, and sugar in a large bowl and keep aside.
- Take fish and rinse it properly and pat dry it with the help of a paper towel. Cut it in a square shape.
- Put the fish in the marinade mix and coat it thoroughly.
- Keep it in the marinade mix for about 20-30 minutes.
- Now let us prepare tofu.
- Drain tofu and dry it with the help of a paper towel. Make a thick layer of tofu on a flat surface. Pat dry and let it drain for 5 minutes.
- Take a steamer and pour 1 to 3-inch water into it and make it ready for steaming. Put a steaming rack over it above 1 inch of water at least. Cover the pot and bring it to boil over high heat.
- While water is boiling, you can cut tofu in half in length. After that cut each half of tofu in a rectangle and it should be a ½ inch in thickness.
- Now lay tofu in a single layer in 9 to 10-inch heat resistant glass pie pan. Layer only what can fit on the glass pie pan.
- Take the fish and lay on top of the tofu and pour marinade on top of it.
- Add ginger on top of it.
- Set a sauté pan on rack and cover and steam until the fish cooks nicely from the center. If possible, taste and check if it is ready. It can take 6 to 8 minutes to cook.
- Once the fish has steamed well, stop steaming and take the sauté pan out from the steamer.
- Sprinkle green onions over it and serve hot.

Nutritional value:

Calories: 240 | Carbohydrate: 5.9 g | Protein: 30 g | Fiber: 0.5g |
Fat: 10g | Cholesterol: 36 mg | Sodium: 780mg

10. Green Fish Curry-Thai Style

Preparation: 10 minutes | Cooking: 20 minutes | Servings: 4

Ingredients:

- Whitefish fillets - ½ pound
- Basmati rice – 8 ounces
- Rice wine – 1 teaspoon
- Green curry paste – 3 tablespoons
- Broccoli- 1 head
- Black sesame seeds- 1 teaspoon
- Coconut milk- 2 cups
- Sweet chili sauce -1 tablespoon
- Carrot -1 unit
- Salt – to taste
- Water – 1 cup

- Soya sauce – 2 teaspoons
- Olive oil – 2 tablespoons
- Water – as required

Cooking directions:

- Take a medium sauté pan, pour coconut milk, water and salt, and make it boil.
- Add basmati rice, cover it and stir and reduce the heat to low. Cook this mixture for at least 15 minutes and remove the pan from the heat and again cover it for 10 minutes until the rice is ready and water absorbed into it. The total liquid content should not be more than 16 ounces (double the quantity of rice), including water and coconut milk.
- While the rice is cooking, mix Thai green curry paste with olive oil in a medium bowl and put pepper and pinch of salt into it, stir well.
- Take white fish fillets and gently coat with the curry paste. You can coat the curry paste high or low as per your choice.
- Cut the broccoli in the length of 2 cm florets. After that chop the stalk roughly.
- Now chop the carrot into ¼" slice.
- Take a small bowl and mix sweet chili sauce, soya sauce, rice wine and keep it aside.
- Pay attention to the rice cooking. Make sure it has enough liquid. When the liquid dries up the rice should be cooked well.
- Now, take a frying pan and drizzle some olive oil for frying and when the pan become hot add broccoli, carrot and some water to cook.
- Stir it well and cook for 5 to 6 minutes.
- Season this mixture with salt and pepper and transfer it in a plate and keep covered.

- Take another pan and drizzle olive oil in it and add fish fillets and cook it for 2-3 minutes. Flip sides so that it will have even cooking.
- Once the rice cooking is over, transfer the coconut rice to a serving plate.
- On top of the rice place the vegetables and fish curry fillets. Further to this, garnish plate with sesame seeds and sweet chili sauce and enjoy hot and delicious food.

Nutritional value:

Calories: 507| Carbohydrate: 56.7 g | Protein: 38.6 g | Sugars: 18g | Fat: 12.7g| Cholesterol: 36 mg | Sodium: 1500mg

ASIAN MAIN DISH RECIPES

1. AMERICAN TANGY BRAISED PORK CHOPS

Preparation: 20 minutes | Cooking: 120 minutes | Servings: 6

Ingredients:

- Pork chops: 1½ to 2 lbs.
- Rice wine: ¼ cup
- Water: 2 cups
- Lemon juice and grated rind: 1
- Worcestershire sauce: ¼ cup
- Chopped onion: 1
- Tabasco drops: Few drops
- Ketchup: 1 cup
- Chopped celery: 2 sticks
- Chili powder: 1 teaspoon

- Brown sugar: ¼ cup
- Salt: to taste (1 teaspoon approximate)

Cooking directions:

- In a medium bowl, mix all the ingredients, excluding pork.
- Put the mixture in a saucepan and bring to boil in low heat for about 10-15 minutes.
- Now put the pork in a baking container and bake it until it becomes brown.
- Pour the mixture over the pork and bake for about 2 hours at 350 degrees Fahrenheit.
- Serve hot.

Approximate Nutritional values:

Calories: 417 | Carbohydrate: 27g | Protein: 35g | Fat: 18g | Cholesterol: 104mg | Sodium: 602mg | Fiber: 1g | Calcium: 102mg

2. CHINESE BRAISED PORK CHOPS

Preparation: 20 minutes | Cooking: 20 minutes | Servings: 4

Ingredients:

- Pork chops: ½ lb.
- Shredded onion: 1 small

For Marinade mix:

- Soy sauce light: 1 tablespoon
- Shaoxing rice wine: 1 tablespoon
- Sugar: ½ teaspoon
- Sesame oil: one pinch
- Corn flour: ½ tablespoon
- White pepper: a pinch
- Salt: to taste

Seasoning:

- Tomato ketchup: ½ tablespoon
- Sugar: 2 teaspoons
- Light soy sauce: 1 teaspoon
- Worcestershire sauce: ½ teaspoon
- Water: 3 tablespoons

Cooking directions:

- Clean the pork in running water.
- Cut the pork to slices and mix it well with the marinade. Leave it to rest for 15 minutes. Tenderize the pork before marinating.
- In a large pan pour 3-4 tablespoons of oil.
- When the oil becomes hot, put the pork chops into the pan.
- Heat the pork until it becomes golden brown.
- Transfer the pork to a plate and drain the oil.
- Now in a saucepan, pour tablespoons of oil and heat on medium temperature.
- Put the sliced onion and cook until it becomes light brown.
- Add seasoning mixture to the pan.
- Now put the cooked chops to the pan and continue cooking until the sauce becomes thick.
- Remove to a serving bowl.
- Serve hot.

Approximate Nutritional values:

Calories: 626 | Carbohydrate: 26g | Fat: 31g | Protein: 58g | Cholesterol: 171mg | Sodium: 373mg | Dietary Fiber: 2g | Calcium: 128mg

3. CHINESE STEAK

Preparation: 10 minutes | Cooking: 15 minutes | Servings: 6

Ingredients:

- Ground beef: 1½ pounds
- Sliced mushrooms: 3-4 ounces
- Grated onion: 2 tablespoons
- Crushed marjoram leaves: ½ teaspoon
- Mushroom gravy mix: 1 envelope
- Red wine: 2 tablespoons
- Pepper: ⅛ teaspoons
- Salt: 1 teaspoon

Cooking directions:

- Mix beef, grated onion, marjoram leaves, pepper, and salt in a large bowl.
- Cut and slice the meat into 6 parts in oval-shaped patties.

- Heat the Salisbury steak for 3-4 minutes on both the sides. Each side may take about 4 minutes.
- Prepare gravy mix as per the instruction on the cover.
- Heat and stir the mushrooms with rice wine.
- Transfer the gravy over the patties.
- Serve hot along with potatoes.

Nutritional value:

Calories: 374 | Carbohydrate: 18g | Protein: 36g | Fat: 16g | Cholesterol: 104mg | Sodium: 1574mg | Dietary Fiber: 1g | Calcium: 53mg

4. Korean Bibimbap

Preparation: 30 minutes | Cooking: 10 minutes | Servings: 6

Ingredients:

- Small pieces of mushrooms: 12 0unces
- 1-inch pieces of firm tofu: 8 0unces
- Rice wine: 2 tablespoons
- Sesame oil: 6 teaspoons
- Soy sauce: ¼ cup
- Rice vinegar: 3 tablespoons
- Grated ginger: 1 tablespoon
- Carrots (shredded): 1 cup
- Bean sprouts: 1 cup
- Chopped scallions: 2-3
- Sesame seeds – 1 tablespoon
- Minced garlic: 2 cloves

- Spinach: 6 ounces
- Eggs: 6
- Salt: to taste
- Cooked brown rice (short grains preferable): 6 cups

For the Sauce:

- Red miso: ½ cup
- Chili garlic sauce: ½ cup

Cooking directions:

- Set the temperature of the oven at 400 degrees Fahrenheit.
- Place mushroom and tofu on the baking sheet.
- In a medium bowl put one teaspoon sesame oil, rice wine, soy sauce, two tablespoons of rice vinegar and ginger. Combine the mixture thoroughly.
- Mix the sauce with mushrooms and tofu and let it coat thoroughly.
- Roast it carefully for 20 minutes at 400 degrees Fahrenheit until it becomes crisp.

<u>Making homemade Gochujang sauce:</u>

- Take another medium bowl and combine carrots, bean sprouts with one teaspoon sesame oil, scallions, and rice vinegar and keep it aside.
- In another small bowl, make gochujang sauce by combining and blending miso and chili sauce.
- In a large pan, heat one teaspoon sesame oil in a medium temperature and add minced garlic, spinach and sauté the ingredients carefully until it gets cooked and set aside.
- Now in large pan pour two teaspoons of sesame oil and heat on medium-high temperature.
- Add eggs and fry it until the whites become firm and yolks fleshy.

Preparing rice bowls:

- Get separate six rice bowl and serve them with the topping of carrots, bean sprouts, mushrooms, tofu, fried eggs, wilted spinach, etc.
- Serve hot with gochujang sauce.

Nutritional value:

Calories: 620| Carbohydrate: 87g | Protein: 27g | Sugar: 25g | Fat: 20g |Fiber: 11g | Cholesterol: 180mg | Sodium: 1730mg

5. ASIAN SALISBURY STEAK

Preparation: 30 minutes | Cooking: 10 minutes | Servings: 4

Ingredients:

- Grounded beef: 12 ounces
- Shao Hsing rice wine: ½ cup
- Diced red bell pepper: ¾ cup
- Hoisin sauce: 4 tablespoons
- Chopped scallions: ¾ cup
- Dry breadcrumbs: ¼ cup
- Canola oil: 3 teaspoons
- Trimmed watercress: 4 bunches
- Fresh ginger: 2 tablespoons
- Salt: to taste

Cooking directions:

- Preheat the oven and grill. Keep the rack in the upper third position of the oven and before preheating, spray coat some cooking oil on the broiler and rack.
- Combine beef, scallions, hoisin sauce, bell pepper, breadcrumbs, and ginger in a medium bowl.
- Add salt to taste.
- Make 4 patties with the mixture and keep it in the grill.
- Spread a teaspoon oil on the patties.
- Broil it and flip as required until it cooked well. It will take approximately 8 minutes.
- Heat a large pan with a few drops of oil and add watercress.
- Stir it for 2-3 minutes.
- Once done, transfer the watercress in four plates.
- Now heat the skillet and pour rice wine, balance hoisin sauce and continue stirring until it becomes smooth and starts bubbling.
- Heat it for about one minute and let it become thick slightly.
- Serve the dish by topping Salisbury steak on top of watercress.
- Spread the sauce on top.

Nutritional value:

Calories: 305 | Carbohydrate: 18g | Protein: 21g | Fat: 13g |Cholesterol: 56mg |Dietary fiber: 2g |Potassium: 623mg | Sodium: 392mg

6. Beef Tenderloin -Asian Style

Preparation: 30 minutes | Cooking: 20 minutes | Servings: 4

Ingredients:

- Mignon filet steaks: 8 ounces
- Shiitake mushrooms: ½ cup
- Rice wine: 2 tablespoons
- Olive oil: 4 tablespoons
- Unsalted Butter: 3 tablespoons
- Minced ginger, fresh: 2 tablespoons
- Minced garlic – 1 tablespoon
- Unsalted butter: ½ cup
- Chopped garlic chives: 2 teaspoons
- Kosher Salt: to taste
- Pepper: as required

Cooking directions:

- Heat the oven at 400 degrees Fahrenheit.
- Season the fillet steaks with salt and pepper.
- Take an oven-safe skillet and pour olive oil.
- Heat until it starts smoking.
- Sear steaks for about 3 minutes per side, until it becomes brown.
- Now put the seared steaks to the preheated oven.
- Bake it for about 10 minutes.
- Once the cooking over, keep it aside warm.
- Now let us make the sauce.
- Take a saucepan and heat 3 tablespoons of butter.
- Add minced ginger and garlic.
- Continue heating for about 2 minutes until it becomes soft start producing the fragrance.
- Put the shiitake mushrooms.
- Add salt to taste and continue cooking for about 4 minutes.
- Add rice wine and sim.
- Continue heating until it reduces to half.
- Now put the remaining butter and continue heating in medium-low temperature.
- When the butter becomes golden brown, stop heating further.
- Season the sauce with pepper and salt.
- Add chives.
- Serve the steaks hot with sauce on top.

Nutritional value:

Calories: 816.47 | Carbohydrate: 5.18g | Protein: 64.91g | Fat: 56.05g | Cholesterol: 260.86mg |Sodium: 481.45mg

7. CHICKEN PICCATA – ITALIAN STYLE

Preparation: 10 minutes | Cooking: 15 minutes | Servings: 4

Ingredients:

- Boneless, skinless chicken breasts: 4
- Flour: for dredging
- Olive oil: 2 tablespoons
- Rice wine: ½ cup
- Lemon Juice: 1/4 cup
- Water: ¼ cup
- Capers drained: 1 tablespoon
- Unsalted butter (¼ inch slice): 3 tablespoons
- Parsley chopped (Italian): 2 tablespoons
- Cayenne pepper: to taste
- Salt: as required

- Black pepper: to taste

Cooking directions:

- Take two plastic wraps.
- Put the chicken breasts between the plastic wraps and bind it in ½ inch thick.
- Now season the chicken with salt, black pepper, and cayenne pepper.
- Then dust with flour.
- Heat a pan in medium flames and add olive oil.
- When the oil becomes hot put chicken in and cook for about 5 minutes. Continue cooking, flip sides until both sides become brown.
- Once done, remove and keep it aside.
- Now cook capers for 30 seconds by pouring oil in another pan. Smash them slightly and let them release the brine.
- Take a clean skillet and pour in rice wine.
- Continue heating until the quantity reduces to half.
- Add water, butter and lemon juice in the same pan for 2 minutes.
- Sir continuously and let it form a thick consistency.
- Add parsley and stir well.
- Add chicken breasts in the pan and heat it for 2-3 minutes.
- Serve by pouring the sauce over the chicken.

Approximate Nutritional value:

Calories: 321 | Carbohydrate: 8.4g | Protein: 24.7g | Fat: 18.2g | Cholesterol: 87mg | Sodium: 224mg |Potassium: 259mg | Dietary fiber: 0.4g |Sugars: 1g

8. Korean Lemon Garlic Chicken

Preparation: 15 minutes | Cooking: 30 minutes | Servings: 4

Ingredients:

- Olive oil: 1 tablespoon
- Skinless, boneless chicken thighs – 2 pounds
- Rice wine: 2 tablespoons
- Chicken stocks – 1½ cups
- Diced yellow onion – ½ medium
- Minced garlic – 3 cloves
- Fresh thyme: 3-5 sprigs
- Lemon – 1 large
- Chopped spinach – 1 cup
- Salt – to taste

- Pepper – as required

Cooking directions:

- Set the oven to 400 degrees Fahrenheit and preheat before cooking.
- Take an oven friendly pan.
- Pour olive oil and heat on medium temperature.
- When the pan becomes hot, put the chicken into the pan and sear both sides. Each side will take 4-5 minutes for searing.
- Remove the chicken to a plate until it becomes golden brown.
- In the same pan add onion and garlic.
- Sauté in low-medium temperature until the onion becomes soft.
- Now put the thyme springs leaves to the pan mixture.
- Pour rice wine and combine the mix well.
- Add pepper and salt to taste.
- Now pour the lemon juice into the mixture.
- Add spinach and chicken stock to the mixture.
- Continue cooking in low heat.
- Check the consistency of the mixture. It should not be too dry.
- Now put the seared chicken into the pan.
- Pour some chicken broth over the chicken.
- Now cover the pan and place it in the oven at 400 degrees Fahrenheit and cook for about 15-20 minutes.
- Serve hot.

Nutritional value:

Calories: 356 | Carbohydrate: 8.1g | Protein: 47.8g | Fat: 14g |Cholesterol: 215.9mg | Sugars: 2.5g |Sodium: 351.8mg

9. Chicken and Veg Fried Rice – Asian Style

Preparation: 10 minutes | Cooking: 10 minutes | Servings: 4

Ingredients:

- Chopped chicken breasts - 8 oz.
- Rice wine - 1 tablespoon
- Brown rice – 2 cup
- Diced onion – 1
- Diced zucchini – 1
- Ear corn (kernels removed) – 1
- Green peas: 1 cup
- Cooked edamame - ½ cup
- Egg – 1
- Broccoli, cooked, chopped in small florets – 2 cup
- Sesame oil – 1 tablespoon

- Soy Sauce – 2 tablespoons
- Minced scallions – 1 cup

Cooking directions:

- Heat a large pan and spray some non-stick cooking oil.
- When the pan becomes hot, put the chicken pieces and sauté until it becomes brown on both sides.
- Once it is done, remove it to a plate and set aside.
- Add and cook onion and zucchini for 3-4 minutes in the same pan.
- Add and stir peas, broccoli, and edamame and corn kernels for 2 minutes and set aside.
- Add the egg, scramble it and stir carefully.
- Add the cooked rice, chicken, oil altogether until it gets brown color for 2 minutes and leaves it for 2 minutes again.
- Add rice vinegar and soy sauce and mix it well.
- Serve hot.

Approximate Nutritional value:

Calories: 357 | Carbohydrate: 47.9g | Protein: 25g | Fat: 8.6g |Cholesterol: 75mg | Sodium: 164mg |Fiber: 8.8g

10. Spicy Beef and Bell Pepper Stir Fry Chinese Style

Preparation: 10 minutes | Cooking: 10 minutes | Servings: 4

Ingredients:

- Canola Oil - 1 tablespoon
- Rice wine - 1½ tablespoons
- Flank steak (diced diagonally) - 12 ounces
- Red bell pepper (fine stripes) - 1
- Yellow bell pepper (finely striped) - 1
- Soy sauce - 3 tablespoons
- Minced ginger - 1 tablespoon
- Chili garlic sauce - 2 teaspoons
- Green onions (chopped) - 4
- Sesame seeds (toasted) - 2 teaspoons

Cooking directions:

- Add a teaspoon of oil in a large nonstick pan and heat over medium temperature.
- Once the oil becomes hot, add flank steaks and sear one side. It will take approximately 2 minutes.
- Once done add bell peppers and continue cooking for about 2 minutes, until the meat changes its pink color.
- Remove the beef into a plate and keep aside.
- In a clean nonstick pan, add chili garlic cause, vinegar, soy sauce, and ginger and cook until it boils.
- Continue cooking until the consistency thickens.
- Now add the flank mixture and chopped onion to the pan.
- Combine it properly and cook for 2-3 minutes
- Once done remove to a serving bowl.
- Garnish with sesame seeds.
- Serve hot.

Nutritional value:

Calories: 216 | Carbohydrate: 7.7g | Protein: 20.8g | Fat: 3.1g | Fiber: 2.2g |Cholesterol: 35mg |Sodium: 480mg | Calcium: 54mg

Asian Salads

1. Asian Cabbage Salad

Preparation: 10 minutes | Cooking: 10 minutes| Servings: 8

Ingredients:

- Canola Oil - 1 tablespoon
- Rice wine - 1½ tablespoons
- Flank steak (diced diagonally) - 12 ounces
- Red bell pepper (fine stripes) - 1
- Yellow bell pepper (finely striped) - 1
- Soy sauce - 3 tablespoons
- Minced ginger - 1 tablespoon
- Chili garlic sauce - 2 teaspoons

- Green onions (chopped) - 4
- Sesame seeds (toasted) - 2 teaspoons

Cooking directions:

- Add a teaspoon of oil in a large nonstick pan and heat over medium temperature.
- Once the oil becomes hot, add flank steaks and sear one side. It will take approximately 2 minutes.
- Once done add bell peppers and continue cooking for about 2 minutes, until the meat changes its pink color.
- Remove the beef into a plate and keep aside.
- In a clean nonstick pan, add chili garlic cause, vinegar, soy sauce, and ginger and cook until it boils.
- Continue cooking until the consistency thickens.
- Now add the flank mixture and chopped onion to the pan.
- Combine it properly and cook for 2-3 minutes
- Once done remove to a serving bowl.
- Garnish with sesame seeds.
- Serve hot.

Nutritional value:

Calories: 216 | Carbohydrate: 7.7g | Protein: 20.8g | Fat: 3.1g | Fiber: 2.2g |Cholesterol: 35mg |Sodium: 480mg | Calcium: 54mg

2. Bacon-Broccoli Salad – American Style

Preparation: 5 minutes | Cooking: 2 minutes|
Servings: 6

Ingredients:

- Broccoli, cut into small pieces- 1 bunch
- Mayonnaise - ¾ cup
- Chinese Rice wine - 2 tablespoons
- Stevia - 3 packets
- Bacon, crisply cooked and chopped no sugar) - 6 slices
- Grated cheddar cheese - ½ cup
- Chopped onion - ¼ cup
- Roasted sunflower seeds - ¼ cup

Preparing directions:

- Steam the broccoli in low heat for about a minute or two in a bowl.
- Drain it in a separate bowl and let it cool.
- Take a large bowl and mix Chinese rice wine, mayonnaise, and stevia.
- Whisk them altogether.
- Now, toss the cheddar cheese and broccoli all over the dressing.
- The salad is ready to serve.

Nutritional value:

Calories: 390 | Total Fats: 36g| Carbs: 9g | Protein: 9g | Dietary fiber: 3g | Cholesterol: 36mg | Potassium: 418mg | Sodium: 416mg | Sugars: 2g

3. Cranberry, Avocado, Orange Glazed Walnut & Blue Cheese Salad-American Style

Preparation: 5 minutes | Cooking: 5 minutes|
Servings: 4

Ingredients:

- Mixed salad greens along with spinach - 1 package (5.5 ounces)
- Rice wine: 4 tablespoons
- Dried and sweetened cranberries - ¾ cup
- Glazed walnuts - ¾ cup
- Drained mandarin oranges - 1
- Crumbled blue cheese - ¾ cup
- Diced, peeled and pitted avocado - 1
- Cranberry vinaigrette salad - 2 tablespoons

Preparing directions:

- Put the salad green into a large salad bowl

- Sprinkle dried cranberries over them, along with mandarin orange sections, walnuts, blue cheese and with avocado chunks.
- Drizzle rice wine.
- Drizzle the salad by adding more of the dressing, until you find it enough.
- Keep tossing the salad bowl to let them mix well together.
- Serve fresh.

Nutritional value:

Calories: 505 | Total Fats: 29.8g| Carbs: 54.3g | Protein: 10.7g | Dietary fiber: 3g | Cholesterol: 19mg | Sodium: 585mg | Potassium: 581mg | Sugars: 28g

4. CHINESE RICE NOODLE SALAD

Preparation: 20 minutes | Cooking: 10 minutes| Servings: 1

Ingredients:

- Cooked rice noodle - ²/₃ cup
- Thinly sliced carrots - ¼ cup
- Thinly sliced zucchini - ¼ cup
- Bean sprouts - ¼ cup
- Black sesame seeds - 1 teaspoon
- Rice wine - 3 tablespoon
- Soy sauce - 2 tablespoon
- Sesame seed oil - 2 tablespoon
- Minced garlic - ½ teaspoon
- Grated ginger - ¼ teaspoon
- Brown sugar - 1 teaspoon

- Salt - to taste

Preparing directions:

- In a large bowl and mix sesame oil, rice wine, soy sauce, grated ginger, minced garlic, salt, and brown sugar.
- Toss the veggies along with the rice noodles in another bowl.
- Drizzle the dressing from the top and mix them well together.
- Before serving, garnish with black sesame seeds.

Nutritional value:

Calories: 355.1 | Total Fats: 5g| Net Carbs: 72.4g | Protein: 8.6g | Fiber: 3g | Potassium: 933mg

5. Radish, Lotus stem, Spring Onion Salad – Chinese Style

Preparation: 30 minutes | Cooking: 5 minutes|
Servings: 2

Ingredients:

- Radish finely sliced - ½ cup
- Spring onions, chopped - ½ cup
- Spinach, blanched spinach - 1 cup
- Lotus stem, cut (tender) - 2/3 cup
- Orange juice - 7 tablespoons
- Rice wine - 3 tablespoons
- Brown sugar - 1 tablespoon
- Chopped red chili - 1
- Sesame oil - 2 tablespoons

- Pickled ginger - 6 slices
- Salt - to taste

Preparing directions:

1. Take a large bowl and add rice wine, orange juice, red chili, brown sugar, sesame oil, pickled ginger, and salt.
2. Mix them altogether
3. Toss the vegetables in a different bowl and then spread it on top of the large bowl kept ready first.
4. Mix them well before serving.

Nutritional value:

Calories: 340 | Total Fats: 5g| Carbs: 72.4g | Protein: 8g | Fiber: 3g | Potassium: 900mg

ASIAN SOUPS

1. NAPA CABBAGE SOUP CHINESE STYLE

Preparation: 5 minutes | Cooking: 25 minutes|
Servings: 4

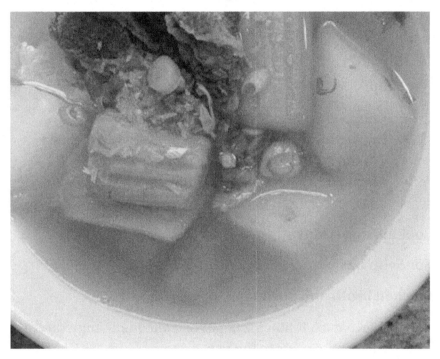

Ingredients:

For Soup base:

- Ginger julienned - 2 large
- Green onions, chopped – 4
- Bacon, chopped - ¼ cup
- Chicken stock – 2 cups

For Meatballs:

- Ground turkey - ½ pound
- Shaoxing wine - 1 tablespoon
- Green onion, finely chopped - ¼ cup
- Soy sauce - 2 teaspoons
- Potato starch - 2 teaspoons
- Ginger, minced - 1 teaspoon
- Egg - 1 large
- Sesame oil - 1 teaspoon
- Salt - ¼ teaspoon

For Soup:

- Chopped Napa cabbage leaves – 8 cups
- Enoki mushrooms - 1 batch (remove the solid ends)
- Daikon radish, chopped - 2 cups
- Chopped black soft tofu - 14 ounces
- Salt - as required to taste

Cooking directions:

For Soup Base:

Chicken broth and pork:

- Preheat a 3.8-liter sized pot on a medium temperature.
- Add bacon parts to the pan.
- When they stop sizzling, reduce the heat from medium to low
- Continue stirring until the bacon turns golden brown.
- Now, add the lean bacon to the pot and continue stirring.
- Pour the chicken stock into the pot and quickly scrape the brown bits stuck in the pot with a spatula.
- Add two cups of water, green onion, and ginger

- Boil the soup by covering for five minutes under high temperature.

Meatballs:

- Combine the meatball ingredients in a large bowl.
- Stir it to become a runny type of mixture.
- Keep it aside for 5-10 minutes.

Soup:

- While the stock simmers, rinse and chop the veggies.
- Put daikon radish into the boiling soup.
- Cover it and cook for about five minutes
- Now put the thick portion of Napa cabbage into the soup.
- Cover and cook for five minutes.
- Put the green parts of Napa cabbage, along with Enoki mushroom into the boiling soup.
- Let it cook for about two to three minutes.
- Add salt to taste.
- After adding salt, put the soft tofu and push the ingredients towards one side of the boiling pot.
- By this way, you can clear up some space for the meatballs for boiling.
- Scoop about 1 to 1.5 tablespoons of meatball texture and add the same to the soup.
- Repeat this scooping process, until you have made fifteen meatballs.
- Cover the pot and simmer it to cook the meatballs for about five minutes
- After five minutes, turn off the heat and remove the cooking pot from the stove, by keeping it covered with the lid.
- Your soup is ready.
- Serve hot.

Approximate Nutritional value:

Calories: 222 | Total Fats: 11g| Carbs: 11.7g | Protein: 23.6g | Fiber: 2g | Cholesterol: 104mg |Sodium: 1078mg |Sugars: 4.2g |Potassium: 695mg

2. INSTANT POT CHICKEN SOUP-US STYLE

Preparation: 5 minutes | Cooking: 20 minutes|
Servings: 6

Ingredients:

- Olive oil - 2 tablespoon
- Celery, sliced - 2 large
- Rice wine - ½ cup
- Skinless chicken breast - 1 pound
- Sliced carrots - 3 large
- Diced onion - 1 large
- Thinly sliced mushrooms - 1 cup
- Minced garlic - 2 cloves
- Dried parsley - 1 teaspoon
- Dried rosemary - 1½ teaspoon

- Wild rice blend - 1 cup
- Corn starch - 3 tablespoons mixed with ½cup of water
- Chicken stock - 4 cups
- Salt - ½ teaspoon

Cooking directions:

- Preheat the instant pot and then pour olive oil.
- Once the oil starts to simmer, put chopped onions, carrots, celery, and the mushrooms.
- Keep stirring for about three minutes or until the vegetables become soft.
- Add rosemary, parsley, and minced garlic to the cooking pot and stir for about one minute.
- Pour rice wine along with the wild rice in the pot
- Add cornstarch mixture, chicken and stock
- Cover the pot and let it cook for about five minutes on high flame.
- After five minutes, bring down the flame to low and remove the lid
- Now carefully take out the chicken breasts from the pot and transfer them to a cutting board.
- Make use of a fork or a knife to cut down the chicken breast into small pieces and then put them back into the boiling soup pot.
- Taste the soup and season it with salt and pepper
- To bring in an extra bit of enhanced flavor, add two to three tablespoons of rice wine to the soup at the end.

Nutritional value:

Calories: 310 | Total Fats: 8g| Carbs: 33g | Protein: 24g | Dietary fiber: 3g | Cholesterol: 48mg | Sugars: 4g | Sodium: 181mg | Potassium: 801mg

3. Chicken Soup with Bok Choy-Japanese Style

Preparation: 10 minutes | Cooking: 30 minutes| Servings: 4

Ingredients:

For Soup Base:

- Chicken broth – 5 cups
- Freshly peeled ginger – 6 slices
- Crushed garlic cloves – 3
- Green onion – 1

For Chicken Udon Soup:

- Shiitake mushrooms – 3½ ounces
- Rice wine - ¼ cup
- Canola oil – 1 tablespoon
- Sliced carrots – ½ cup
- Freshly peeled and minced ginger – 2 teaspoons
- Minced garlic – 1 clove

- Soy sauce – 1 tablespoon
- Shredded and cooked chicken breast – 1 pound
- Black pepper – as required
- Kosher salt – as per your taste
- Udon noodles – 15 ounces
- Boiled egg – 8 slices
- Green onions - ¼ cup
- Baby Bok choy – 10 ounces

Cooking directions:

For Soup Base:

- Remove the stems from the mushrooms and keep it aside.
- Thinly slice down the mushroom button and keep them aside as well.
- Combine the chicken broth, mushroom stems, crushed garlic, ginger slices and green onions in a large saucepan.
- Bring to boil at high temperature.
- Once the soup starts to boil, cover the saucepan with a lid and reduce the heat and let the soup boil for about twenty minutes.
- Turn down the heat and let the saucepan stay covered for about ten minutes
- By using a slotted spoon, remove all solids from the soup.
- Strain the stock using a sieve placed over a bowl and completely discard the solids.

For Chicken Udon Soup:

- Take a large saucepan and heat it on a medium high temperature.
- Pour canola oil into the saucepan and swirl to coat all over the pan.
- When the oil becomes hot, put sliced carrot, mushrooms and sauté for about two minutes.

- Add the minced garlic and ginger and sauté it for about one minute
- Now pour rice wine into the saucepan and let it cook for about four minutes
- Meanwhile, scrape the pan to loosen the stuck brown bits.
- Pour the strained stock into the saucepan and bring it to boil.
- Once it starts boiling, reduce the heat to medium
- Add pepper, soy sauce followed by Bok choy and shredded chicken into the saucepan.
- Simmer it for about two minutes or until the chicken gets thoroughly heated.
- Cook the Udon noodles without salt separately and add it to the soup.

Nutritional value:

Calories: 461 | Total Fats: 13g| Carbs: 21g | Protein: 58g | Fiber: 2g | Cholesterol: 139mg | Sodium: 397mg | Potassium: 82mg | Sugars: 2g

CHICKEN WILD RICE SOUP-AMERICAN STYLE

Preparation: 10 minutes | Cooking: 40 minutes| Servings: 14

Ingredients:

- Chicken broth – 2 quarts
- Rice wine - ½ cup
- Cubed cooked chicken – 2 cups
- Freshly chopped mushrooms - ½ pound
- Celery, finely chopped – 1 cup
- Carrots, shredded – 1 cup
- Finely chopped onion - ½ cup
- Chicken bouillon crumbs – 1 teaspoon
- Parsley flakes (dried) – 1 teaspoon
- Garlic powder - ¼ teaspoon
- Dried thyme - ¼ teaspoon

- Butter - ¼cup
- All-purpose flour - ¼ cup
- Undiluted condensed cream of mushroom soup - 1 can
- Cooked wild rice - 3 cups

Cooking directions:

- Take a large pan and add chicken broth, chopped mushrooms, celery, carrots, onions, chicken bouillon granules, and parsley flakes.
- Bring to boil on high temperature.
- Once the soup starts boiling, reduce the heat to low and cover it.
- Let the soup boil for the next thirty minutes
- Melt butter in a Dutch oven.
- Once the butter has melted, add flour.
- Keep stirring the flour until it turns smooth.
- Now, gradually whisk in the broth mixture.
- Bring it to boil.
- Keep stirring it for about two minutes or until it becomes thickened
- Whisk in wine and soup.
- Add chicken and rice and heat it.

Nutritional value:

Calories: 154 | Fats: 6g| Carbohydrates: 14g | Protein: 10g | Fiber: 2g | Cholesterol: 27mg | Sugars: 2g | Sodium: 807mg

5. KETO CHICKEN SOUP-INDIAN STYLE

Preparation: 10 minutes | Cooking: 20 minutes| Servings: 6

Ingredients:

- Cooked and diced chicken - 16oz
- Unsalted chicken broth or bone broth - 6 cups

For the vegetable base:

- Avocado oil, olive oil or butter - 4 tablespoons
- Rice wine - ¼ cup
- Celery root - 8 ounces
- Sliced celery - 1 cup
- Diced onion - ½ cup
- Carrot - ⅓ cup
- Sliced garlic - 1 large clove
- Lemon zest - 1 teaspoon
- Whole bay leaf - 1

- Garlic herb seasoning blend - 1 tablespoon
- Chicken base (granulated, paste or bouillon) - 2 teaspoons
- Pepper and salt – as required to taste.

Cooking directions:

- Dice the vegetables and chicken.
- Take a four-quart pot and preheat it on a high flame
- Once the pot turns hot, add either butter or oil to it.
- Add all the mentioned vegetables, bay leaf and lemon zest to the pot.
- Keep stirring the ingredients to let them mix well one over another.
- Reduce the heat to medium and then add the garlic herb seasoning blend, wine, and the chicken base.
- Keep stirring for about two minutes.
- Cover the pot and let the vegetables cook for about three to four minutes on medium heat.
- Later, add chicken broth to the pot and bring it to a boil.
- Once the soup starts boiling, reduce the heat to low and check the tenderness of the vegetables using a fork.
- If the vegetables are thoroughly cooked and tender, then it is time to add chicken to it.
- Add salt and pepper as per your taste and serve it hot.

Nutritional value:

Calories: 274 | Total Fats: 15g| Carbs: 8g | Protein: 26g | Fiber: 2g

HOMEMADE RICE WINE RECIPES

Wine is one of the popular beverages in the world, and people consume it during functions and special occasions. In certain functions, people do keep a special wine session to augment the celebration and for honoring the guests. But wine is not just only a drink. It has been used in preparing delicious foods and as a taste enhancer. The wines used for cooking are cooking wines, and there are many types of cooking wines available on the market.

The rice wine becomes rice wine vinegar once exposed to air. When it is exposed to oxygen, the fermentation process converts the alcohol content of the wine into acetic acid, and it changes to rice wine vinegar. Therefore, if you want to have the original quality of rice wine, you have always to use fresh rice wine.

Rice wine is a preferred ingredient for cooking in most of the Asian countries like China and Japan. It is known as Sake in Japan and Shaoxing Wine in China. Rice Wine is a critical ingredient which adds a unique flavor to the recipes. A specific amount of alcohol in the rice wines are the signature tastes of different parts of the world, mostly used in the Asian countries.

Most of the countries in the world use cooking wine for food preparation. In East Asian countries and China, rice wines are used commonly, by fermenting the starch of rice. In the USA and Europe, grapes are used to make cooking wine.

Types of Rice Wine as per the Countries:

1. **Sake** – A Japanese Rice Wine is a bit lighter in taste with a sweet-dry flavor and is an ideal substitute for Chinese rice wine. It contains 15% of alcohol in the beverage.

2. **Shaoxing Wine** – It is a Chinese Rice Wine which is also known as **Shaosing Wine**, adds a salty flavor to the recipes.

3. **Tapai / Brem** – The Indonesian / Southeast Asian Rice Wine is a mild sweet in taste. The much lesser amount of alcohol adds a flavor of tanginess in the recipes.

4. **Tuak and Lihing** – These are Malaysian Rice Wines popular in Sabah (Lihing) and Sarawak (Tuak) states. It is an essential ingredient in the Malaysian recipes.

5. **Makgeolli** – It is a Korean Rice Wine Beverage. A mixture of sweet, sour, milky and alcoholic flavor is a favorite beverage amongst the Koreans.

COOKING RICE WINE

Ingredients:

- Sticky or Glutinous Rice – 2 cups
- Wine Yeast Ball – 1

Cooking directions:

- Use rinsed rice.
- Rinse two cups of rice three times or until the rice washing water becomes clear.
- Put the rinsed rice in hot water for one hour. Keeping it in hot water helps to cook the rice better.
- Strain the rice.
- Boil 2 cups of water in a medium rice cooking steamer pot.
- When the water starts boiling, place the rice in the upper compartment of the steamer and close the lid.
- Continue steaming it for 25 minutes.
- Ensure the rice does not touch the boiling water.
- Make sure to cook the rice thoroughly.
- Once cooking is over, stop cooking.
- Now spread the rice on a cooking sheet so that it can cool down quickly.
- Let it cool down. Now we can move to the fermentation part.
- Take a large bowl and break the yeast into powder.
- Spread the crushed pieces of yeast over the cooked rice and mix it well.
- Put the mixture into another airtight container and store it. Heat it in a low temperature of 100 degrees Fahrenheit

or put a heating pad around the container for a few days. The heat will act as a catalyst for fermentation.

- Observe and taste the accumulated wine at the bottom of the container.
- Keep the container in a warm place for a month.
- If you let it ferment for a more extended period, it will change the taste. It will become more smooth, sweet and less effervescent.
- After a month's fermentation, the wine will be ready for consumption. By using a cheesecloth or a strainer, you can filter the wine and keep in a bottle and refrigerate.
- Always tightly close the lid, if not the wine will become rice wine vinegar.
- Refrigeration will help to extend the life of rice wine.
- After a few days of refrigeration, if you happen to find sediments in the wine, you can remove it, which can improve its appearance.
- Your wine is ready to use in the recipes or as a drink.

Nutritional value:

Calories: 234 | Carbohydrate: 8.7g | Protein: 0.9g | Fat: 0g |Potassium: 44mg |Sodium: 3.5mg |Cholesterol: 0 mg | Dietary fiber: 0 mg

Alcoholic Rice Wine 'Sake'

Ingredients:

- Rice – 2½ pounds
- Corn Sugar – 2½ pounds
- Grape concentrate – 8 oz.
- Hot Water – 14 cups
- Acid blend – 3 teaspoons
- Yeast nutrient – ¾ teaspoon
- Sherry yeast – 1 package
- Campden tablet – 1

Cooking directions:

- Rinse rice 3-4 times until the water becomes clean.
- Crush the rice well.
- Take a fermentation container and put the crushed rice along with grape concentrate in a straining bag by knotting the top. A nylon straining bag is preferable.
- Pour hot water and other ingredients in the container carefully. Set aside for 48 hours.
- Add yeast nutrient and stir the mixture daily for a few days and press the pulp lightly and check its specific gravity.
- After reaching the gravity at 1.050, you can add ¼ pound corn sugar liquid. Its specific gravity may reach to 1.050 after 2 or 3 days.
- In 6 to 7 days the gravity may fall to 1.030 and when the gravity reaches to this level, drain the juice to another airtight container.
- Again, add ¼pound corn sugar liquid/gallon when the gravity reaches to 1.020.

- Check the gravity regularly and when the specific gravity reaches 1.000 or less, which is the indication of completion of fermentation, you can transfer the molasses to another clean airtight container.
- Transfer the liquid to another clean airtight container every two months, so that the molasses remain clean.
- Your SAKE is almost ready.
- When the fermentation is complete, you can bottle the wine.
- If you need to increase the alcohol content in the wine, try adding more sugar before the fermentation process complete.
- If you want to sweeten the SAKE, add ½ teaspoon stabilizer and ¼ pound corn sugar liquid/gallon.
- Bottle it and use.

Approximate Nutritional values:

Calories: 38.9 | Carbohydrate: 1.5g | Protein: 0.1g | Fat: 0g | Cholesterol: 0g |Potassium: 7.2mg |Sodium: 0.6mg

CONCLUSION

At the end of the day, people will only think about the luscious and flavorful taste of your Asian rice wine dishes that you served them. But this is not the end. This limited edition of the recipe book also includes information on the delectable rice wine preparation process and various cuisine recipes. The book will also give you some basic understanding of various rice wines available in different parts of the world. In this book, we have simplified the cooking procedures and also included the most commonly available groceries for your convenience.

We hope you will have a wonderful session of cooking with rice wine which will be a unique experience and that you will enjoy the Asian rice wine recipes.

Made in the USA
Las Vegas, NV
22 April 2021